THE GOSPEL PROJECT FOR KIDS

The Gospel Project for Kids: Older Kids Leader Guide

JERUSALEM REBUILT, JOHN THE BAPTIST, AND JESUS' EARLY YEARS

© 2014 LifeWay Press®. Reprinted January 2015.

No part of this work may be reproduced or transmitted in any form or by any means, electronic or mechanical, including photocopying and recording, or by any information storage or retrieval system, except as may be expressly permitted in writing by the publisher. Requests for permission should be addressed in writing to LifeWay Press®, One LifeWay Plaza, Nashville, TN 37234-0172.

ISBN: 978-1-430033-72-1
Item 005665552

Dewey Decimal Classification Number: 220.07
Subject Heading: BIBLE—STUDY\THEOLOGY—STUDY\GOSPEL—STUDY

Printed in the United States of America

W9-BJH-455

CONTENTS

Suggested for use the week of:

Unit 22: Jerusalem Was Rebuilt

_____ Session 1: Nehemiah Heard News of Jerusalem — 2

_____ Session 2: Jerusalem's Walls Rebuilt — 18

_____ Session 3: Ezra Read the Law — 34

_____ Session 4: Malachi the Prophet — 50

Unit 23: The Forerunner of the Savior

_____ Session 1: Genealogy of Christ — 66

_____ Session 2: John's Birth Was Predicted — 82

_____ Session 3: Mary Visited Elizabeth — 98

_____ Session 4: John Was Born — 114

Unit 24: God's Plan Is Jesus

_____ Session 1: Jesus Was Born — 130

_____ Session 2: Jesus Was Dedicated — 146

_____ Session 3: Jesus at the Temple — 162

_____ Session 4: Jesus Was Baptized — 178

_____ Session 5: Jesus Was Tempted — 194

_____ Session 6: Jesus Called Disciples — 210

Kids Ministry Publishing
LifeWay Church Resources
One LifeWay Plaza
Nashville, Tennessee 37234-0172

We believe that the Bible has God for its author; salvation for its end; and truth, without any mixture of error, for its matter and that all Scripture is totally true and trustworthy. To review LifeWay's doctrinal guidelines, please visit *www.lifeway.com/doctrinalguideline*.

Unless otherwise noted, all Scripture quotations are taken from the Holman Christian Standard Bible®, copyright 1999, 2000, 2002, 2003, 2009 by Holman Bible Publishers. Used by permission.

Unit 22: JERUSALEM WAS REBUILT

Unit Description:

God brought a faithful remnant of His people back home. He used Nehemiah to protect His people by leading them to rebuild the city walls. The people returned to God when Ezra read the law and revealed their sin. Though the people grieved their sin, they rejoiced in the joy of the Lord. God sent Malachi, the final Old Testament prophet, to tell the people of a coming messenger who would prepare the way for Jesus, the final Messenger. (*4 sessions*)

Unit 23: THE FORERUNNER OF THE SAVIOR

Unit Description:

God's plan to send the promised Messiah to earth was coming together. An angel announced to Zechariah that his wife, Elizabeth, was going to have a baby named John. Elizabeth's relative Mary was also expecting a child—Jesus, the Son of God. Even in the womb, John rejoiced over Jesus' presence. God appointed John the Baptist to be the forerunner of the Savior. (*4 sessions*)

Unit 24: GOD'S PLAN IS JESUS

Unit Description:

After Jesus was born in Bethlehem, He grew up and began to prepare for His ministry. Jesus demonstrated from a young age that He understood His role as God's Son. When Jesus was baptized, God confirmed His sonship. Jesus was subsequently tempted by Satan, but He did not sin. As Jesus' ministry began, He called twelve men to follow Him in His mission of bringing salvation to the world. (*6 sessions*)

Leader BIBLE STUDY

After the Babylonian exile, God's people were known as Jews—people from the kingdom of Judah. Nehemiah was a Jew living in Persia. He served as the king's cupbearer, a position of great trust; the cupbearer made sure no one poisoned the king's drink. Sometimes the cupbearer even tasted some of the drink himself to ensure its potability.

When the Persian Empire conquered the Babylonians, King Cyrus allowed God's people to return to Judah. Two or three million Jews had originally been deported, but only a remnant—50,000 people—returned. They set up their homes and rebuilt God's temple in Jerusalem. Nehemiah's story takes place after Ezra led a second group of exiles back to Judah.

Nehemiah received word about God's people who had returned to Judah. They were in trouble and living in shame; the walls of Jerusalem were broken down, and the city gates were burned. They lived in fear, unprotected from their enemies. Nehemiah sat down and wept.

Nehemiah fasted and prayed for days. He remembered God's promise to His people. Their disobedience led to exile, but if they turned back to the Lord, their obedience would lead to blessing. God promised to restore their fortunes and give His people a home. (See Deut. 30:1-10.)

The king noticed Nehemiah's sadness, and Nehemiah was afraid. No one was supposed to be sad in the presence of the king; it was an insult to his greatness. Nehemiah explained the plight of his city. The king granted him leave and gave him letters to ensure his safe passage. Nehemiah arrived in Jerusalem. He encouraged the people to rebuild the walls and stood confidently against opposition.

This story is the beginning of Nehemiah's work to rebuild the walls of Jerusalem. As you teach kids, point out that Nehemiah trusted God's promise to give His people a home. When we repent and trust in Jesus, we can trust His promise to prepare a place for us in His Father's house, where we will be with Him forever. (See John 14:3.)

Older Kids BIBLE STUDY OVERVIEW

Session Title: Nehemiah Heard News of Jerusalem
Bible Passage: Nehemiah 1–2
Big Picture Question: What did Nehemiah want to do? Nehemiah wanted to rebuild Jerusalem's walls.
Key Passage: Malachi 4:2
Unit Christ Connection: God restored a faithful remnant and reminded them of His promise of a new covenant through Jesus Christ.

Small Group Opening

Welcome time ....Page 6
Activity page (5 minutes)..Page 6
Session starter (10 minutes) ....Page 6

Large Group Leader

Countdown ....Page 8
Introduce the session (3 minutes) ....Page 8
Timeline map (1 minute)..Page 9
Big picture question (1 minute) ....Page 9
Tell the Bible story (9 minutes) ....Page 10
The Gospel: God's Plan for Me (optional) ....Page 10
Key passage (5 minutes) ....Page 11
Discussion starter video (5 minutes)..Page 11
Sing (4 minutes)...Page 12
Prayer (2 minutes)..Page 12

Small Group Leader

Key passage activity (5 minutes) ....Page 14
Bible story review & Bible skills (10 minutes)................................Page 15
Activity choice (10 minutes)..Page 16
Journal and prayer (5 minutes) ....Page 17

The BIBLE STORY

Nehemiah Heard News of Jerusalem
Nehemiah 1–2

Nehemiah (NEE huh MIGH uh) **was a Jew, one of God's people.** God's people had lived in Babylon for many years until King Cyrus let them go home. Some of God's people went home to Judah, but some of them stayed in Babylon. Soon, the king of Persia took over Babylon. He became the new king. **Nehemiah** stayed and **worked for the king of Persia.**

One day, some men came from Judah. Nehemiah asked, "How are God's people doing in Jerusalem?"

The men had bad news. "The people are in trouble. They are ashamed. **The walls around Jerusalem are broken down**, and the gates have been burned down."

When Nehemiah heard this, he sat down and cried. Nehemiah prayed and fasted for several days. "Yahweh, God," he prayed, "let Your eyes be open and Your ears hear my prayer. We have sinned against you. Please remember Your words to Moses: 'If you are unfaithful, I will scatter you among the peoples. But if you return to Me and obey Me, I will gather you from the ends of the earth and bring you to the place I have chosen.' Please, Lord, hear my prayer."

Nehemiah went back to serving the king, but he was still sad. The king noticed Nehemiah's mood and **asked Nehemiah, "What's wrong? Why are you sad?"**

Nehemiah was afraid; no one was supposed to be sad around the king. **Nehemiah told the king, "The city where my ancestors are from is in trouble.** It is in ruins, and the gates of the city have been burned down."

"What do you want to do?" the king asked.

Before Nehemiah answered the king, he prayed. Then **Nehemiah said, "Please send me to Jerusalem so I can rebuild the city."**

The king agreed to send Nehemiah to Jerusalem. He gave Nehemiah letters to keep him safe as he traveled. If anyone tried to stop him, Nehemiah could show that he had the king's permission to go to Jerusalem. Also, the king made sure Nehemiah had wood to help rebuild the city gates and wall. He even sent some men from his army to protect Nehemiah.

Nehemiah arrived safely in Jerusalem. He didn't tell anyone why he was there. After three days, Nehemiah got up in the middle of the night and went to look at the city's walls. Then **he told the people there, "We are in trouble.** The city is ruined, and the gates have been burned down. **Come, let's rebuild Jerusalem's wall."**

Nehemiah told the people how God had helped him, and he told them everything the king had said and done. **The people said, "Let's start building," and so they did.**

Christ Connection: Nehemiah trusted that God would keep His promise to protect His people and give them a home. When we trust in Jesus, we have a home in heaven with God. Jesus obeyed God perfectly. He died on the cross and rose again so we can have a home with Him forever in heaven.

Small Group OPENING

Session Title: Nehemiah Heard News of Jerusalem
Bible Passage: Nehemiah 1–2
Big Picture Question: What did Nehemiah want to do? Nehemiah wanted to rebuild Jerusalem's walls.
Key Passage: Malachi 4:2
Unit Christ Connection: God restored a faithful remnant and reminded them of His promise of a new covenant through Jesus Christ.

Welcome time

Greet each kid as he or she arrives. Use this time to collect the offering, fill out attendance sheets, and help new kids connect to your group.

Ask kids to share their favorite places to travel or to which places they would like to travel.

Activity page (5 minutes)

- "Missing Letters" activity page, 1 per kid
- pencils

Challenge kids to complete the king's letter on the "Missing Letters" activity page. Instruct them to fill in the blanks to discover who traveled to Jerusalem. Explain that traveling long distances could be dangerous in Bible times.

Say • A man named Nehemiah wanted to travel from Persia to the city of Jerusalem. The king of Persia gave him a letter to make sure he arrived safely.

Session starter (10 minutes)

Option 1: Nothing but trouble

- action figure or balloon with eyes and a frown drawn on it

Guide kids to sit in a circle. Display the prop and introduce it as Henry. Explain that Henry had a very bad day. Invite kids to help you tell the story of Henry's bad day. Kids will pass Henry around the circle, each adding to Henry's experience. After a kid describes an event, he should add, "Just when Henry thought it couldn't get any worse … " and then pass Henry to the next kid.

Start the story by saying, "Today, Henry woke up late. Just when Henry thought it couldn't get any worse … " and then pass Henry around the circle. If a kid struggles to provide a scenario, ask, "What went wrong next?" Continue the story until everyone takes a turn.

Say • What can you do when you are having a bad day? Sometimes talking to your parents about it can help you feel better. You can also pray! God is in control, and you can ask Him for help. In our Bible story today, a man named Nehemiah was having a bad day.

Option 2: I can help!

• facial tissues or napkins

Instruct kids to scatter around the room. Give each kid a facial tissue to position on the top of her head. Challenge kids to move across the room, keeping the tissues on their heads. If a player's tissue falls off her head, she must freeze. Another player should approach the frozen player and say, "I can help!" and then position the tissue back on her head.

Direct kids to move in different ways: walking slowly, walking quickly, hopping, skipping, tiptoeing, and so forth.

Say • Today we are going to hear a Bible story about a man named Nehemiah. Nehemiah worked for the king of Persia. Some of Nehemiah's friends and family members were living in Jerusalem. Nehemiah heard that they were in trouble, and he was sad. The king of Persia saw Nehemiah was sad. Do you know what the king said? "How can I help?"

Transition to large group

Jerusalem Was Rebuilt

Large Group LEADER

Session Title: Nehemiah Heard News of Jerusalem
Bible Passage: Nehemiah 1–2
Big Picture Question: What did Nehemiah want to do? Nehemiah wanted to rebuild Jerusalem's walls.
Key Passage: Malachi 4:2
Unit Christ Connection: God restored a faithful remnant and reminded them of His promise of a new covenant through Jesus Christ.

• room decorations

Tip: Select decorations that fit your ministry and budget.

Suggested Theme Decorating Ideas: Simulate a rock climbing wall by hanging a gray sheet or tablecloth. Cut round pieces from various colors of construction paper and attach them to the sheet to resemble handholds and footholds. Display climbing tools such as a helmet, backpack, gloves, compass, carabiner clips, and ropes.

Countdown

• countdown video

Show the countdown video as your kids arrive, and set it to end as large group time begins.

Introduce the session (3 minutes)

• backpack

[Large Group Leader enters wearing a backpack.]
Leader • Hi, everyone! Today is a great day to do some climbing. I have to be honest with you, though. I'm not a very experienced climber. I mean, I watched some how-to videos on the Internet, but this is actually my first time, and I don't think I'm quite ready.

Oh, please excuse me for not introducing myself. My name is *[your name]*. I'm really glad you're here. We are going to learn all about rock climbing. If you know a lot already, great! If you've never even seen a rock before … well, it is helpful if you know what a rock is. But we're all here to learn. One of the most important things about rock climbing is your gear. You need to have the right equipment to climb safely.

[*Open backpack and turn it upside down.*] Oh, dear. It's empty. I seem to have forgotten to bring the most important things! When you are in a dangerous situation, you absolutely must have the right tools to protect yourself.

Timeline map (1 minute)

• Timeline Map

Display the timeline map where kids can see it. As you introduce the Bible story, point to it on the timeline map.

Leader •Well, since we can't get started climbing just yet, I'll tell you today's story. It's from the Bible. Everything in the Bible is true, so this story really happened! It's about some of God's people who were in trouble—people who needed to be protected! Let's see now. What is the name of today's story? Ah, here it is. The story is called "Nehemiah Heard News of Jerusalem."

Well, that is interesting. I wonder what kind of news Nehemiah heard. Good news or bad news? What do you think?

Big picture question (1 minute)

Leader •That's not the only question I have today. We have a big picture question to figure out. Our big picture question is, ***What did Nehemiah want to do?*** Boy, this must have been important news; it made Nehemiah want to do something about it.

Tell the Bible story (9 minutes)

• "Nehemiah Heard News of Jerusalem" video
• Bibles, 1 per kid
• Bible Story Picture Slide or Poster
• Big Picture Question Slide or Poster

Tip: A Bible story script is provided at the beginning of every session. You may use it to guide you as you prepare to teach the Bible story in your own words. For a shorter version of the Bible story, read only the bolded text.

Open your Bible to Nehemiah 1 and tell the Bible story in your own words, or show the Bible story video "Nehemiah Heard News of Jerusalem."

Leader • Nehemiah heard that the people in Jerusalem were in trouble. The people in Jerusalem were God's people. Nehemiah was probably friends with many of them. Maybe he had family members there. This news made Nehemiah sad. Nehemiah wanted to help them!

Nehemiah worked for the king, and no one was supposed to be sad around the king. But Nehemiah couldn't help it. The king asked him what was wrong.

Do you remember our big picture question? *What did Nehemiah want to do? Nehemiah wanted to rebuild Jerusalem's walls.* Say that with me. *What did Nehemiah want to do? Nehemiah wanted to rebuild Jerusalem's walls.*

The king could have said no, but Nehemiah prayed and asked God for help. The king allowed Nehemiah to go. He even helped him get to Jerusalem safely with the supplies he needed. Nehemiah inspected the walls, and the people agreed to rebuild the walls so their homes would be safe.

Nehemiah trusted that God would keep His promise to protect His people and give them a home. Jesus obeyed God perfectly. He died on the cross and rose again. When we trust in Jesus, we have a home with Him forever in heaven.

The Gospel: God's Plan for Me (optional)

Using Scripture and the guide provided, explain to boys and girls how to become a Christian. Tell kids how they can respond, and provide counselors to speak with each kid individually. Guide counselors to use open-ended questions to allow kids to determine the direction of the conversation.

Encourage boys and girls to ask their parents, small group leaders, or other adults any questions they have about becoming a Christian.

Key passage (5 minutes)

- Key Passage Slide or Poster
- "Celebrate" song

Leader • Our key passage is from the Book of Malachi. Let's find the Book of Malachi in the Bible. Malachi was a minor prophet. Remember, that doesn't mean he wasn't important. It's just that his book isn't very long. We will hear the story about Malachi later.

Help kids find the Book of Malachi in their Bibles. Lead them to read the key passage aloud.

Leader • Does anyone know what it means to fear God's name? This type of fear isn't like being afraid of heights or hairy spiders. Fearing God's name means you understand who God is. God is holy, and He always does what is right. It means respecting Him and knowing He would be right to punish you for your sin.

Our key passage says that God has good news for people who understand who He is. We will learn more about that news later.

Lead the group to repeat the entire verse aloud together. Sing "Celebrate."

Discussion starter video (5 minutes)

- "Unit 22 Session 1" discussion starter video

Leader • So according to our big picture question and answer, *What did Nehemiah want to do? Nehemiah wanted to rebuild Jerusalem's walls.* When Nehemiah heard the bad news, he took action. How do you respond to bad news? Check out this video.

Show the "Unit 22 Session 1" video.

Leader • Do those reactions look familiar? Does receiving

bad news make you feel afraid or hopeless? Do you ever
pray to God when you are worried? Why or why not?
Allow kids to share their answers honestly. Remind them
that bad news can make us sad, but we can trust God to take
care of us.

Sing (4 minutes)

• "We Won't Be
Shaken" song

Leader • What did Nehemiah do when he got the bad news
about God's people in Jerusalem? Yes, he was sad, but
he also prayed and asked God for help. And God helped
him! God was in control. The king could have refused to
let Nehemiah go to Jerusalem, but the Bible says God was
gracious to Nehemiah.

God is so good! He gives us favor when we don't
deserve it. I think that's a great reason to praise Him. Will
you sing our theme song with me?

Lead boys and girls to sing "We Won't Be Shaken."

Prayer (2 minutes)

Leader • I am so glad you came today to learn some of the
basics of rock climbing. Will you come back next week?
Oh, wonderful! I'll be sure to remember my safety gear.
Now, one more time: *What did Nehemiah want to do?*
Nehemiah wanted to rebuild Jerusalem's walls. Great
job. Before you go to your small group, I am going to
pray.

Close in prayer. Thank God for comforting us when we hear
bad news. He is Lord over everything, and we can trust Him
to work out everything for our good.

Dismiss to small groups

The Gospel: God's Plan for Me

Ask kids if they have ever heard the word *gospel*. Clarify that the word *gospel* means "good news." It is the message about Christ, the kingdom of God, and salvation. Use the following guide to share the gospel with kids.

God rules. Explain to kids that the Bible tells us God created everything, and He is in charge of everything. Invite a volunteer to read Genesis 1:1 from the Bible. Read Revelation 4:11 or Colossians 1:16-17 aloud and explain what these verses mean.

We sinned. Tell kids that since the time of Adam and Eve, everyone has chosen to disobey God. (Romans 3:23) The Bible calls this sin. Because God is holy, God cannot be around sin. Sin separates us from God and deserves God's punishment of death. (Romans 6:23)

God provided. Choose a child to read John 3:16 aloud. Say that God sent His Son, Jesus, the perfect solution to our sin problem, to rescue us from the punishment we deserve. It's something we, as sinners, could never earn on our own. Jesus alone saves us. Read and explain Ephesians 2:8-9.

Jesus gives. Share with kids that Jesus lived a perfect life, died on the cross for our sins, and rose again. Because Jesus gave up His life for us, we can be welcomed into God's family for eternity. This is the best gift ever! Read Romans 5:8; 2 Corinthians 5:21; or 1 Peter 3:18.

We respond. Tell kids that they can respond to Jesus. Read Romans 10:9-10,13. Review these aspects of our response: Believe in your heart that Jesus alone saves you through what He's already done on the cross. Repent, turning from self and sin to Jesus. Tell God and others that your faith is in Jesus.

Offer to talk with any child who is interested in responding to Jesus.

Small Group LEADER

Session Title: Nehemiah Heard News of Jerusalem
Bible Passage: Nehemiah 1–2
Big Picture Question: What did Nehemiah want to do? Nehemiah wanted to rebuild Jerusalem's walls.
Key Passage: Malachi 4:2
Unit Christ Connection: God restored a faithful remnant and reminded them of His promise of a new covenant through Jesus Christ.

Key passage activity (5 minutes)

• Key Passage Poster
• sticky notes
• marker

Use one sticky note per kid. Write one or more words of the key passage on each sticky note.

Direct kids to form a circle around a table or on the floor, cross each arm with the kid's arm next to them, and lay their hands flat.

Attach the prepared sticky notes in the correct order to the back of the kids' hands. Prompt the player with the first word of the passage to pat her hand on the floor and say the first word. Then the player with the next word will pat his hand and say the second word. Players continue patting in order until they say the whole verse.

For an added challenge, instruct kids to start the passage from the beginning each time. The second player will say the first word and his word, the third player will say the first and second words and his word, and so forth. Kids repeat previous words each time until the verse is complete.

Say • Great job, everyone! These are the words God spoke through His prophet Malachi. The Book of Malachi is the last book in the Old Testament. We will learn more about Malachi later.

Bible story review & Bible skills (10 minutes)

- Bibles, 1 per kid
- Small Group Visual Pack

Option: Retell or review the Bible story using the bolded text of the Bible story script.

Help kids find Nehemiah 1–2 in their Bibles. Nehemiah is in the Old Testament, about one-third of the way through the Bible. Demonstrate how to use the table of contents if kids need help finding the Book of Nehemiah. Review the Bible story in your own words, or retell the story using the bolded portions of the Bible story script.

Say • What did Nehemiah do when he heard the news of Jerusalem? (*He sat down, cried, fasted, and prayed; Neh. 1:4*)

• *What did Nehemiah want to do? Nehemiah wanted to rebuild Jerusalem's walls.*

• What did the king give Nehemiah to ensure safe travel? (*letters, Neh. 1:7-8*)

• When did Nehemiah inspect Jerusalem's walls? (*at night, Neh. 2:12-13*)

If you choose to review with boys and girls how to become a Christian, explain that kids are welcome to speak with you or another teacher if they have questions.

• **God rules.** God created and is in charge of everything. (Gen. 1:1; Rev. 4:11; Col. 1:16-17)

• **We sinned.** Since Adam and Eve, everyone has chosen to disobey God. (Rom. 3:23; 6:23)

• **God provided.** God sent His Son, Jesus, to rescue us from the punishment we deserve. (John 3:16; Eph. 2:8-9)

• **Jesus gives.** Jesus lived a perfect life, died on the cross for our sins, and rose again so we can be welcomed into God's family. (Rom. 5:8; 2 Cor. 5:21; 1 Pet. 3:18)

• **We respond.** Believe that Jesus alone saves you. Repent. Tell God that your faith is in Jesus. (Rom. 10:9-10,13)

Activity choice (10 minutes)

- paper
- markers and crayons

Option 1: A safe home

Provide paper, markers, and crayons for each kid. Invite each kid to draw a picture of his home. For an added challenge, suggest that kids draw a map of their streets or neighborhoods. As they work, prompt kids to talk about what they like best about their homes. Allow them to share details they have included in their pictures such as trees or mailboxes. Kids may wish to add drawings of their family members or pets.

Comment that God's people had lived far away in a foreign land for many years, and they had finally returned home. But a home needs to be a safe place. Nehemiah saw that his friends and family members needed help, and he was sad.

Say • *What did Nehemiah want to do? Nehemiah wanted to rebuild Jerusalem's walls.*

• God had promised to protect His people and keep them safe. Nehemiah prayed to God for help, and he trusted God to keep His promises. God has a home for us, too. If we trust in Jesus as Lord and Savior, God has a place for us—a home—with Him in heaven.

Option 2: Protect your home

- table tennis balls, 4 or more
- straws, 1 per kid
- dominoes

Direct four kids to gather around a table. If you have multiple tables, form several groups. If needed, allow kids to play on teams. Give each kid a straw. The goal of this game is for each kid to protect his side of the table, or his "home." Position four or more table tennis balls in the center of the table. Kids should use their straws to blow the table tennis balls away from their homes, back toward the center of the table.

After a few minutes, provide several dominoes for each kid to arrange as a wall across his side of the table. Then kids can play another round.

Point out how much easier defending your home is with a wall to protect you.

Say • *What did Nehemiah want to do? Nehemiah wanted to rebuild Jerusalem's walls.*

• Jerusalem was home to many of God's people. They needed to be protected from their enemies. God was with His people, and He helped Nehemiah travel safely to Jerusalem to rebuild the walls.

Journal and prayer (5 minutes)

• pencils
• journals
• Bibles
• Journal Page, 1 per kid (enhanced CD)
• "A Nighttime Inspection" activity page, 1 per kid

Lead kids to think about something they need help with. Perhaps they need courage to tell a friend about Jesus or they need patience with a sibling.

Encourage each kid to write on the journal page a short prayer asking God for help. Remind them that Nehemiah prayed to God for help.

Say • *What did Nehemiah want to do? Nehemiah wanted to rebuild Jerusalem's walls.*

Invite kids to share prayer requests. Close the group in prayer, thanking Jesus for obeying God perfectly and dying on the cross so we can have a home with Him in heaven. Ask God to comfort kids when they pray for help.

Tip: Each quarter, the *Older Kids Activity Pack* includes a set of *Big Picture Cards for Families*. Give the card pack to parents today to allow families to interact with the biblical content each week.

As time allows, lead kids to complete the activity page "A Nighttime Inspection."

Leader BIBLE STUDY

When the Babylonians took God's people to Babylon, they destroyed Jerusalem. God's people returned years later to rebuild the temple, but when they faced opposition in rebuilding the rest of Jerusalem, they stopped. Some 70 years passed, and the walls and gates around the city were still ruined.

City walls and gates were very important in Bible times. Walls were built to be several feet thick. They protected a city from its enemies and provided a sense of safety and security. Gates were the center of city life, the meeting place for commercial and social transactions. Without these structures, the surviving remnant of God's people struggled and was vulnerable to attack.

Nehemiah traveled from Persia to Jerusalem to lead the effort in rebuilding Jerusalem's walls. Nehemiah's leadership was effective. Nehemiah 3 describes all the people working together to rebuild the gates and walls.

But it wasn't long before Nehemiah met opposition. Sanballat and Tobiah were local governors who strongly opposed Nehemiah's helping the Jews. The two mocked God's people and tried to discourage them. Sanballat and Tobiah planned a surprise attack against God's people, but God's people found out. They kept working—with a trowel in one hand and a sword in the other.

God's people completed the wall in just 52 days. Note how their enemies reacted: "All the surrounding nations were intimidated and lost their confidence, for they realized that this task had been accomplished by our God" (Neh. 6:16).

Now God's people were protected from their enemies. God provided the way for us to be protected from our enemies, sin and death. He sent His Son, Jesus, to die on the cross for our sins. When we repent and trust in Jesus, He frees us from sin and death. We still sin, but we are no longer slaves to sin. (See Rom. 6:17-18.) We will die a physical death as a result of sin, but we have eternal life. (See John 11:25-26; Rom. 6:23.)

Older Kids BIBLE STUDY OVERVIEW

Session Title: Jerusalem's Walls Rebuilt

Bible Passage: Nehemiah 3:1–6:16

Big Picture Question: How did God protect His people? God used Nehemiah to lead the people to rebuild the city walls.

Key Passage: Malachi 4:2

Unit Christ Connection: God restored a faithful remnant and reminded them of His promise of a new covenant through Jesus Christ.

Small Group Opening

Welcome time ....Page 22

Activity page (5 minutes)...Page 22

Session starter (10 minutes) ....Page 22

Large Group Leader

Countdown ....Page 24

Introduce the session (3 minutes) ....Page 24

Timeline map (1 minute)..Page 25

Big picture question (1 minute) ....Page 25

Tell the Bible story (10 minutes) ....Page 25

The Gospel: God's Plan for Me (optional) ....Page 26

Key passage (5 minutes) ....Page 27

Discussion starter video (5 minutes)..............................Page 27

Sing (3 minutes)..Page 27

Prayer (2 minutes)...Page 28

Small Group Leader

Key passage activity (5 minutes) ....Page 30

Bible story review & Bible skills (10 minutes)................Page 30

Activity choice (10 minutes)..Page 32

Journal and prayer (5 minutes) ....Page 33

The BIBLE STORY

Jerusalem's Walls Rebuilt
Nehemiah 3:1–6:16

Nehemiah (NEE huh MIGH uh) **was in Jerusalem to help the people rebuild the city walls. The people started working together to fix the walls and the burned-down gates**. The walls and gates had special names. Some of the people worked on the Fish Gate. The Fish Gate was the entrance to the fish market. Some people worked on the Sheep Gate; this gate led to the place men gathered to sell sheep.

Others worked on the Valley Gate, the Old Gate, and the Horse Gate. The people worked on the walls, and other workers repaired the towers along the walls.

The workers put in doors, bolts, and bars. They cut stones and lifted them into place on the wall, and they filled in gaps and holes. All around the city, people worked side by side. Soon the wall was half as tall as it had once been!

Not everyone was happy that Jerusalem's walls were being rebuilt. **Some men who lived nearby were angry. Sanballat** (san BAL uht) **and Tobiah** (toh BIGH uh) **mocked the people.** Sanballat said, "What do these people think they are doing? These walls are just piles of trash and dirt. They can't be rebuilt!"

Nehemiah prayed. God's people kept working on the walls, but their enemies made a plan to attack them and stop their work. God's people prayed and assigned men to guard the walls all day and all night, but they were discouraged. "Our enemies are everywhere," they said.

Nehemiah reminded the people that God was with them. "Do not be afraid. God is great and powerful!" Nehemiah said. **"Be ready. If our enemies attack us, God will fight for us!"** Sanballat and Tobiah could threaten God's people, but they couldn't make God's people stop building. Sanballat and Tobiah were not in charge of rebuilding the wall; God was!

So God's people went back to work. Some stood guard with weapons, and others worked on the wall. Some men worked with one hand and held a weapon in the other. **They were always ready to fight, just in case.**

Nehemiah was a wise and good leader of God's people while they worked. He helped them solve any problems they had, and he did not give in to their enemies. **The people kept working very hard. In just 52 days, the wall was complete!** The gates were repaired, and the wall was restored. **When all of Jerusalem's enemies heard that the wall had been rebuilt, they were afraid because they knew God was with His people.**

Christ Connection: Nehemiah led the people to rebuild the walls around Jerusalem to protect them from their enemies. Jesus came to protect us from our enemies. He died on the cross and rose from the dead to rescue people from sin and death.

Small Group OPENING

Session Title: Jerusalem's Walls Rebuilt
Bible Passage: Nehemiah 3:1–6:16
Big Picture Question: How did God protect His people? God used Nehemiah to lead the people to rebuild the city walls.
Key Passage: Malachi 4:2
Unit Christ Connection: God restored a faithful remnant and reminded them of His promise of a new covenant through Jesus Christ.

Welcome time

Greet each kid as he or she arrives. Use this time to collect the offering, fill out attendance sheets, and help new kids connect to your group.

Ask kids to describe cool things they have built. What materials did they use? How long did it take to build?

Activity page (5 minutes)

- "Rebuild a Word" activity page, 1 per kid
- pencils

Invite kids to work in pairs or small groups on the activity page "Rebuild a Word." Boys and girls should use the letters in the word *rebuild* to create other words. Each letter may only be used once in a new word. If kids need help, offer some clues: two colors (*blue, red*), a place to sleep (*bed*), a place to buy meat (*deli*), or an animal that flies (*bird*).

Say • Things that are broken down need to be rebuilt. In the Bible story we will hear today, God's people worked to rebuild something they really needed.

Session starter (10 minutes)

Option 1: Stack it up

- craft sticks, 1 per kid
- numbered cubes or pennies, 20 or more

Invite two or three kids to play at a time. Other kids should cheer them on. Instruct each player to place the end of a craft stick in his mouth. When you start the timer, players will begin stacking numbered cubes on their sticks, one at a time. If a cube falls, the player should pick up another and continue stacking. Call time after one minute. Count each player's stack to see who stacked the most cubes.

Play several rounds, allowing other kids a chance to play. Supply a new craft stick to each player.

Say • In our Bible story today, a man named Nehemiah needed wood to repair some gates. The wooden gates in the walls around Jerusalem had been burned down.

Option 2: The power of many

• large cardboard squares, 2
• paper cups

Tip: If the platform does not support a child's weight, use more cups.

Choose a volunteer to stand at the front of the room. Give him two paper cups. Instruct him to stand on the cups without crushing them. It's impossible! Two paper cups are not strong enough to support a child's weight.

Now, give each kid two paper cups. Challenge the group to work together to build a platform that will hold someone's weight. They may only use the paper cups and two cardboard squares. Allow several minutes for kids to work. The platform can be formed by arranging paper cups upside down on a cardboard square. Then position the second square on top of the cups. A kid should be able to stand on the cardboard without crushing the cups.

Say • The cardboard helps distribute—or spread out—your weight. One cup alone can't hold you, but many cups working together can! In our Bible story today, God's people needed to work together to build something that none of them could build alone.

Transition to large group

Large Group LEADER

Session Title: Jerusalem's Walls Rebuilt
Bible Passage: Nehemiah 3:1–6:16
Big Picture Question: How did God protect His people? God used Nehemiah to lead the people to rebuild the city walls.
Key Passage: Malachi 4:2
Unit Christ Connection: God restored a faithful remnant and reminded them of His promise of a new covenant through Jesus Christ.

Countdown

• countdown video

Show the countdown video as your kids arrive, and set it to end as large group time begins.

Introduce the session (3 minutes)

• backpack
• helmet

[Large Group Leader enters wearing a backpack and carrying a helmet. Leader knocks on the helmet.]

Leader • Safety first, safety first! That's what I always say. This is my helmet, and it is absolutely essential for rock climbing. Rock climbers are very careful to use the right equipment to stay safe, but a helmet will protect your noggin if you fall or if a rock falls on you!

So, who's ready to learn about rock climbing today? You are? Well, I am going to teach you everything I know.

Can anyone tell me what else a climber needs to stay safe? *[Pause for responses.]* Yes, those are great suggestions! Climbers need the right shoes, a harness, ropes, a climbing partner, and so forth.

Oh, I can't wait to tell you about today's Bible story! It's all about God's people. They were living in a city that was not safe, but God sent them just what they needed.

Timeline map (1 minute)

• Timeline Map

Use the timeline map to point out and review the previous Bible story "Nehemiah Heard News of Jerusalem."

Leader • Look at our timeline map. Does anyone remember what kind of news Nehemiah heard when he was in Persia? That's right. Nehemiah heard bad news. He was sad because he found out that his friends and family members were living in a city without walls. Walls were very important because they kept the people safe from their enemies. So Nehemiah got permission from the king of Persia to go to Jerusalem and help his people.

Today, we're going to hear how Nehemiah helped protect the people in Jerusalem.

Big picture question (1 minute)

Leader • That leads me to our big picture question. Our big picture question is, *How did God protect His people?* God had promised to protect His people and give them a home. They needed protection from their enemies. God helped Nehemiah get to Jerusalem so Nehemiah could help the people. Listen to the Bible story to find out what happened next.

Tell the Bible story (10 minutes)

• Bibles, 1 per kid
• "Jerusalem's Walls Rebuilt" video
• Bible Story Picture Slide or Poster
• Big Picture Question Slide or Poster

Open your Bible to Nehemiah 3 and tell the Bible story in your own words, or show the Bible story video "Jerusalem's Walls Rebuilt."

Leader • Nehemiah led the people in Jerusalem to rebuild the city walls. He encouraged them, and they trusted God to help them. They worked on different parts of the wall.

But was everyone happy about the wall being rebuilt? No! Sanballat (san BAL uht) did not want the Jews to rebuild Jerusalem's walls. He and his friend Tobiah mocked the people and made fun of them. They hoped God's people would just give up and stop building.

When people are mean and discouraging, sometimes we just want to give up. But what did Nehemiah do? Well, first he prayed. That's always a great place to start. Nehemiah told God that the people felt discouraged, and he asked God to punish Sanballat and Tobiah. Then, God's people got back to work. They were always ready to defend themselves, just in case.

Nehemiah was a good leader. The people finished the wall, and their enemies knew the only way they could have done that was because God was with them.

How did God protect His people? God used Nehemiah to lead the people to rebuild the city walls. That's our big picture question and answer. Say it with me. *How did God protect His people? God used Nehemiah to lead the people to rebuild the city walls.*

Do we have enemies today? Some people are against us. Some people do not like God or the good news about Jesus. Our greatest enemies, though, are sin and death. Everyone is a sinner, and we deserve to die for our sin. Guess what! Jesus came to protect us from our enemies. He died on the cross and rose from the dead to free us from sin. When we trust in Him, we will live with Him forever in heaven.

The Gospel: God's Plan for Me (optional)

Use Scripture and the guide provided to explain to boys and girls how to become a Christian. Tell kids how they can respond, and provide counselors to speak with each kid individually. Encourage boys and girls to ask their parents, small group leaders, or other adults any questions they have about becoming a Christian.

Key passage (5 minutes)

• Key Passage Slide or Poster
• "Celebrate" song

Leader • Our key passage is from the Book of Malachi. Let's read it together.

Lead kids to read Malachi 4:2. Allow any kids who have memorized the passage to recite it from memory.

Leader • Does anyone know who the sun of righteousness is? Good guesses! The prophet Malachi was talking about Jesus! What does a sun do? It shines and lights up the darkness. It also warms things that are cold. In the New Testament, the apostle John wrote that Jesus is the light that shines in the darkness. (John 1:5)

Sing "Celebrate."

Discussion starter video (5 minutes)

• "Unit 22 Session 2" discussion starter video

Leader • God loved His people in Jerusalem, and He promised to protect them. Let's answer our big picture question. ***How did God protect His people? God used Nehemiah to lead the people to rebuild the city walls.*** Speaking of protection, do you think God protects His people from *every* bad thing? Let's watch this video.

Show the "Unit 22 Session 2" video.

Leader • When you are injured or get sick, does that mean God is not with you or that He doesn't love you? What do you think?

Allow kids to share their ideas. Reassure them that God will never stop loving them, and He will never leave them. Because of sin, everyone will face suffering on earth until Jesus comes and makes all things right.

Sing (3 minutes)

• "We Won't Be Shaken" song

Leader • We've seen how God protected His people in Jerusalem by sending Nehemiah to help rebuild the city walls. Rebuilding the walls wasn't easy because some of the men nearby made fun of God's people and didn't want them to rebuild the walls. These enemies even made a plan to attack God's people. God's people had to be ready to fight. Do you remember what Nehemiah told them? He said, "God will fight for us!"

Let's praise God for being a God who protects His people. He is worthy of our praise. Sing our theme song with me.

Lead boys and girls to sing "We Won't Be Shaken."

Prayer (2 minutes)

Leader • *How did God protect His people? God used Nehemiah to lead the people to rebuild the city walls.* You know, people still suffer on earth today. God allows suffering, but He protects us from the greatest threat. The Devil wants us to turn away from God, and he will do anything he can to get us to stop loving God. Did you know that Jesus prayed for us when He was on earth? He asked God to protect us from the Devil. (John 17:15) That makes me feel so safe. That's ultimate protection.

Let's pray, and then you can go to your small groups. God, thank You for giving ultimate protection to those who trust in Jesus. Lord, we confess that we do not always turn to You when we are suffering and hurting. Help us to trust You when life is hard. We know that You are good, and one day You will send Jesus back to make everything right.

Dismiss to small groups

The Gospel: God's Plan for Me

Ask kids if they have ever heard the word *gospel*. Clarify that the word *gospel* means "good news." It is the message about Christ, the kingdom of God, and salvation. Use the following guide to share the gospel with kids.

God rules. Explain to kids that the Bible tells us God created everything, and He is in charge of everything. Invite a volunteer to read Genesis 1:1 from the Bible. Read Revelation 4:11 or Colossians 1:16-17 aloud and explain what these verses mean.

We sinned. Tell kids that since the time of Adam and Eve, everyone has chosen to disobey God. (Romans 3:23) The Bible calls this sin. Because God is holy, God cannot be around sin. Sin separates us from God and deserves God's punishment of death. (Romans 6:23)

God provided. Choose a child to read John 3:16 aloud. Say that God sent His Son, Jesus, the perfect solution to our sin problem, to rescue us from the punishment we deserve. It's something we, as sinners, could never earn on our own. Jesus alone saves us. Read and explain Ephesians 2:8-9.

Jesus gives. Share with kids that Jesus lived a perfect life, died on the cross for our sins, and rose again. Because Jesus gave up His life for us, we can be welcomed into God's family for eternity. This is the best gift ever! Read Romans 5:8; 2 Corinthians 5:21; or 1 Peter 3:18.

We respond. Tell kids that they can respond to Jesus. Read Romans 10:9-10,13. Review these aspects of our response: Believe in your heart that Jesus alone saves you through what He's already done on the cross. Repent, turning from self and sin to Jesus. Tell God and others that your faith is in Jesus.

Offer to talk with any child who is interested in responding to Jesus.

Small Group LEADER

Session Title: Jerusalem's Walls Rebuilt
Bible Passage: Nehemiah 3:1–6:16
Big Picture Question: How did God protect His people? God used Nehemiah to lead the people to rebuild the city walls.
Key Passage: Malachi 4:2
Unit Christ Connection: God restored a faithful remnant and reminded them of His promise of a new covenant through Jesus Christ.

Key passage activity (5 minutes)

- Key Passage Poster
- index cards, 24
- marker

Write words or phrases of the key passage on 12 separate index cards. Make two matching sets. Mix up all the cards and arrange them facedown on the floor or on a table.

Invite kids to play a concentration-style game. They should match the words of the key passage in order. Players take turns turning over two cards. If a match is made, the player gets another turn. If the cards do not match or are not the next words in the key passage, the player should put the cards back down, and play passes to the next player. If time allows, play several rounds.

Say • You are getting so good at learning the key passage! Remember, fearing God means knowing who God is. God is holy and righteous. And who is the sun of righteousness? Right, Jesus!

Bible story review & Bible skills (10 minutes)

- Bibles, 1 per kid
- Small Group Visual Pack

Provide a Bible for each kid and instruct kids to stand. Guide them to find the Book of Nehemiah in the Bible. When a kid locates the book, she may sit down. Assist any kids who need help.

Review the timeline in the small group visual pack.

Retell or review the Bible story in your own words, or use the bolded text of the Bible story script.

Direct kids to turn to Nehemiah 3 and use the Bible to answer the following questions about the Bible story. For each review question, supply the reference for kids to find the answer.

Say • *How did God protect His people? God used Nehemiah to lead the people to rebuild the city walls.* (*Neh. 2:17*)

• Name one of the three gates with an animal name. (*Fish, Neh. 3:3; Horse, Neh. 3:28; Sheep, Neh. 3:32*)

• How did Sanballat try to discourage God's people? (*He mocked them, Neh. 4:1-2*)

• Who helped the people rebuild the wall? (*God, Neh. 6:16*)

If you choose to review with boys and girls how to become a Christian, explain that kids are welcome to speak with you or another teacher if they have questions.

• **God rules.** God created and is in charge of everything. (Gen. 1:1; Rev. 4:11; Col. 1:16-17)

• **We sinned.** Since Adam and Eve, everyone has chosen to disobey God. (Rom. 3:23; 6:23)

• **God provided.** God sent His Son, Jesus, to rescue us from the punishment we deserve. (John 3:16; Eph. 2:8-9)

• **Jesus gives.** Jesus lived a perfect life, died on the cross for our sins, and rose again so we can be welcomed into God's family. (Rom. 5:8; 2 Cor. 5:21; 1 Pet. 3:18)

• **We respond.** Believe that Jesus alone saves you. Repent. Tell God that your faith is in Jesus. (Rom. 10:9-10,13)

Activity choice (10 minutes)

Option 1: Protect yourself

Invite kids to play an active game. Give each kid two clothespins to attach to the shoulders of her shirt.

Direct kids to move around the room. At your signal, they will try to collect clothespins from other players. A player may not touch or cover her own clothespins. If a player loses both of her clothespins, she is out. Play continues until only one player's clothespin remains attached to her shirt.

Say • Protecting your clothespins was difficult! The other players—your "enemies"—attacked from every direction. ***How did God protect His people? God used Nehemiah to lead the people to rebuild the city walls.***

• The walls around Jerusalem protected God's people from their enemies. God sent Jesus to protect us from our enemies. Even though some people here on earth might act like enemies to us, our true enemies are sin and death. Jesus died on the cross and rose from the dead to rescue people from sin and death.

Option 2: Build a wall

Provide graham crackers and cake frosting or cream cheese. Encourage each kid to use the crackers and cream cheese to build walls or gates. Suggest kids make the tallest gate or longest wall.

As kids work, invite them to retell the Bible story in their own words. Ask them the following questions to recall details of the Bible story:

1. Why was Nehemiah in Jerusalem? (*to help rebuild the city walls, Neh. 2:17*)

2. Who didn't want Jerusalem's walls to be rebuilt?

• spring-hinged clothespins, 2 per kid

• Allergy Alert (enhanced CD)
• graham crackers
• cake frosting or cream cheese
• plastic knives
• paper plates
• ziplock bags

(Sanballat and Tobiah; Neh. 4:1,3)

3. What did God's people do when they were
   discouraged? (*They prayed to God; Neh. 4:4,9*)
4. Whom did Nehemiah say would fight for the
   people of Jerusalem? (*God would fight for them,
   Neh. 4:20*)
5. How many days did it take to rebuild Jerusalem's
   wall? (*52 days, Neh. 6:15*)
6. Who came to protect us from our enemies? (*Jesus
   came to protect us from our enemies. He died
   on the cross and rose from the dead to rescue
   people from sin and death.*)

When kids finish building, they may disassemble their
creations and enjoy them as a snack. Provide ziplock bags
for kids to take home their leftovers.

Say • *How did God protect His people? God used
Nehemiah to lead the people to rebuild the city
walls.*

• God helped His people rebuild the walls around
Jerusalem. The walls were important because they
protected the people from their enemies. God sent
Jesus to protect us from our true enemies. Jesus died
on the cross and rose from the dead to rescue people
from sin and death.

Journal and prayer (5 minutes)

• pencils
• journals
• Bibles
• Journal Page, 1 per
  kid (enhanced CD)
• "Count It Up!"
  activity page,
  1 per kid

Say • Draw or write something that scares you or makes
you worry. Then spend time praying, asking God to
help you trust Him.

Invite kids to share prayer requests. Close the group in
prayer, or allow a couple volunteers to close the group in
prayer. As time allows, lead kids to complete the activity
page "Count It Up!"

Leader BIBLE STUDY

Ezra was a priest in Babylon at the end of the exile. More than 50 years after the first group of exiles to return to Jerusalem had completed and dedicated the temple, Ezra led a second group back to Jerusalem.

Just as God had been with Nehemiah, He was with Ezra—granting him favor with the Persian king. The king gave Ezra permission to go to Jerusalem. He provided Ezra with a letter and access to resources to ensure safe travel. (See Ezra 7:11-26.)

Ezra traveled to Jerusalem with a purpose. God's people had spent 70 years in exile, and they needed to be reminded how to live. As a scribe, Ezra was an expert on the law of Moses, and he had "determined in his heart to study the law of the Lord, obey it, and teach its statutes and ordinances in Israel" (Ezra 7:10).

Under Nehemiah's leadership, the people had rebuilt Jerusalem's walls. They gathered together at the Water Gate to hear the law of Moses. Men, women, and children—anyone who could understand—came to listen to the reading of God's Word.

From early morning until midday, Ezra read from the book of the law of Moses. He stood on a high wooden platform where everyone could see and hear him. Ezra opened the book of the law, and everyone stood up. The Levites helped the listeners understand the words of the law.

The people reacted strongly to hearing and understanding the law of Moses. Verse 9 says the people were weeping. The law revealed their sin.

God's Word is powerful. The law reveals our sin and how short we fall to meeting God's standard. As you teach kids, help them recognize that we cannot meet God's requirements. We need a Savior. God sent Jesus to obey the law perfectly and die for our sins. We can trust in Him for salvation.

Older Kids BIBLE STUDY OVERVIEW

Session Title: Ezra Read the Law
Bible Passage: Nehemiah 8:1-12
Big Picture Question: Why did Ezra read God's Word? God's Word
helped people obey God so they could be holy.
Key Passage: Malachi 4:2
Unit Christ Connection: God restored a faithful remnant and reminded
them of His promise of a new covenant through Jesus Christ.

Small Group Opening

Welcome time ....Page 38
Activity page (5 minutes)..Page 38
Session starter (10 minutes) ....Page 39

Large Group Leader

Countdown ....Page 40
Introduce the session (3 minutes) ....Page 40
Timeline map (2 minutes) ....Page 41
Big picture question (1 minute) ....Page 41
Tell the Bible story (10 minutes) ....Page 41
The Gospel: God's Plan for Me (optional) ....Page 42
Key passage (5 minutes) ....Page 42
Discussion starter video (4 minutes)...Page 43
Sing (3 minutes)...Page 43
Prayer (2 minutes)...Page 44

Small Group Leader

Key passage activity (5 minutes) ....Page 46
Bible story review & Bible skills (10 minutes)................................Page 46
Activity choice (10 minutes)...Page 48
Journal and prayer (5 minutes) ....Page 49

The BIBLE STORY

Ezra Read the Law
Nehemiah 8:1-12

The walls around Jerusalem were finished—at last! The people had worked hard, and with God's help they finished rebuilding the walls and the city gates in just 52 days. **All the people in Jerusalem gathered together very early in the morning at one of the city gates. Men, women, and children—anyone who could understand—came to listen to the reading of God's Word.**

As the sun was just coming up, Ezra (EZ ruh) **the priest brought out the book of the law of Moses that God had given to His people.** God's words were written on a scroll. Ezra stood on a high wooden platform. Some men stood next to Ezra on his right and on his left. Ezra opened the book where everyone could see it.

Ezra began to read. He read the law for several hours, **and all the people listened carefully. All the people stood up. They had respect for God's Word. Ezra praised God, and the people lifted up their hands.**

"Amen! Amen!" they said. **The people in the crowd bowed down with their faces to the ground, and they worshiped God.**

Some of the leaders there—the Levites (LEE vights)—**explained the law to the people and helped them understand the words Ezra read. As the people heard the words of the law, they began to weep.** The law was God's rules for living, and the people had disobeyed God. **They realized they had sinned.**

Ezra, the Levites, and Nehemiah (NEE huh MIGH uh) **the governor said, "This day is holy to the Lord your God. Do not mourn or weep."** Even though the people's sin made them sad, this was a happy day.

Then Ezra said to them, "Go home and prepare a feast! Eat rich food and drink sweet drinks. **Share what you have prepared with those who have nothing prepared."** And again Ezra said, **"Today is holy to the Lord our God. This is not a day to be sad because the joy of the Lord is your strength."**

The people obeyed Ezra. They prepared a feast. They ate rich food and drank sweet drinks. They shared what they had with people who did not have food and drinks, and all the people had a big celebration. **They were glad because they understood the words of the law that were explained to them.**

Christ Connection: God's Word is powerful. When Ezra read God's Word, the people changed their ways and loved God more. The Bible says that Jesus is "the Word." Jesus is God who came to live with people on earth. Jesus has the power to change our hearts.

Small Group OPENING

Session Title: Ezra Read the Law
Bible Passage: Nehemiah 8:1-12
Big Picture Question: Why did Ezra read God's Word? God's Word helped people obey God so they could be holy.
Key Passage: Malachi 4:2
Unit Christ Connection: God restored a faithful remnant and reminded them of His promise of a new covenant through Jesus Christ.

Welcome time

Greet each kid as he or she arrives. Use this time to collect the offering, fill out attendance sheets, and help new kids connect to your group.

Invite kids to talk about their favorite books—either current favorites or favorites when they were younger. Ask them to share the longest amount of time they've ever spent reading a book.

Activity page (5 minutes)

- "On the Books" activity page, 1 per kid
- Bibles, 1 per kid
- pencils

Provide a Bible for each kid and guide kids to complete the activity page "On the Books." Demonstrate how to use the table of contents to locate a Bible book.

Say • God gave His people commands in the Bible about how to live, but after awhile the people stopped obeying God's law. They forgot about God's commands and lived however they wanted.

• God gives us commands to help us. Can you think of some rules or laws we have today that are meant to help us?

Guide kids in a brief discussion. Prompt them to consider safety rules in the classroom or traffic laws on the road.

Session starter (10 minutes)

Option 1: Stand, hands, facedown

Choose a volunteer to stand at the front of the room. Teach kids three positions: *stand*—stand tall with hands at their sides, *hands*—lift hands above their heads, or *facedown*—drop to your knees and bow your face to the ground.

The volunteer will lead. He should shout out a position and assume that pose. The rest of the kids should race to mimic the leader's motion. Allow the leader to take a few turns calling; then he should choose a new leader. Leaders can challenge the class by increasing the speed at which they call out positions.

Say • In today's Bible story, a crowd stood to hear Ezra the priest read God's Word. They praised God by lifting their hands in the air, and they worshiped Him with their faces bowed to the ground.

Option 2: Shadow scenes

• large sheet of paper
• desk lamp
• markers
• tape

Hang a large sheet of paper on a wall. Point a desk lamp toward the paper. Then dim the overhead lights. Invite half the kids to stand between the lamp and the paper to create shadows. Instruct the group to strike a pose and freeze in place. The second group can use markers to trace around the shadows on the paper. When kids have finished tracing the scene, guide groups to switch roles. Then turn on the lights and allow kids to fill in their outlines as time permits.

Say • Shadows happen when an object blocks light—from a source like the sun—from passing through.

• Today we are going to hear a Bible story about God's people. They got up early, when the sun was just coming up, to hear God's Word.

Transition to large group

Large Group LEADER

Session Title: Ezra Read the Law
Bible Passage: Nehemiah 8:1-12
Big Picture Question: Why did Ezra read God's Word? God's Word helped people obey God so they could be holy.
Key Passage: Malachi 4:2
Unit Christ Connection: God restored a faithful remnant and reminded them of His promise of a new covenant through Jesus Christ.

Countdown

· countdown video

Show the countdown video as your kids arrive, and set it to end as large group time begins.

Introduce the session (3 minutes)

· book about rock climbing

[Large Group Leader enters carrying a book about rock climbing.]

Leader • Hi, everyone! Remember me? I'm [*your name*]. It's good to see you today. I've been reading this book about rock climbing, and I'm ready to tell you some of the things I've learned. Last week we learned about rock climbing safety: helmets, climbing partners, ropes, harness, and all sorts of safety things.

We are so close to being ready to climb. But once you get your safety gear on, you need to know what to do. Well, this book says exactly how to climb. You can learn a lot from books! I'm going to show you one of the basic climbing techniques. Everyone, hold your arms straight up in the air. Now curl your fingers forward like you're grabbing onto some handholds in the rock. Great job! Straight arms keep your muscles from getting so tired when you're climbing.

This book is full information so you know just what to do when you're climbing.

Timeline map (2 minutes)

• Timeline Map

Use the timeline map to point out and review the previous Bible stories, "Nehemiah Heard News of Jerusalem" and "Jerusalem's Walls Rebuilt."

Leader • Look at our timeline map. Can anyone remember what we learned about Jerusalem's walls? Yes, good memory. Nehemiah went to Jerusalem to help God's people rebuild the walls. God's people worked together, and they finished the walls so they were protected from their enemies.

Big picture question (1 minute)

Leader • Today we are going to hear a Bible story about a priest named Ezra. After the walls were rebuilt, Ezra read God's Word to the people. I wonder why he did that. Our big picture question is, *Why did Ezra read God's Word?* We'll hear why during the Bible story. Listen carefully to figure out the answer.

Tell the Bible story (10 minutes)

• "Ezra Read the Law" video
• Bibles, 1 per kid
• Bible Story Picture Slide or Poster
• Big Picture Question Slide or Poster

Open your Bible to Nehemiah 8. Tell the Bible story in your own words, or show the video "Ezra Read the Law."

Leader • When the walls around Jerusalem were rebuilt, the people got up very early in the morning. They stood near one of the gates, and Ezra read God's law to them.

Remember, God gave His law to Moses after He rescued the Israelites from slavery in Egypt. The law showed the Israelites how to live and that God requires people to obey Him perfectly. The people had promised to follow God's laws.

Let's look again at our big picture question. *Why did Ezra read God's Word? God's Word helped the people obey God so they could be holy.* Say that with me. *Why did Ezra read God's Word? God's Word helped the people obey God so they could be holy.*

When Ezra read the law, the people cried because they realized they had disobeyed God. Ezra told the people to celebrate and be happy. Yes, they had sinned and needed God's forgiveness, but God's plan was to save them.

We all disobey God. Nothing we do can earn our own salvation. Nothing we do is good enough. But God sent Jesus to save us. Jesus obeyed God perfectly. He died on the cross, taking the punishment for our sins. Jesus rose from the dead. When we trust in Him, God forgives our sins completely.

The Gospel: God's Plan for Me (optional)

Using Scripture and the guide provided, explain to boys and girls how to become a Christian. Tell kids how they can respond, and provide counselors to speak with each kid individually. Guide counselors to use open-ended questions to allow kids to determine the direction of the conversation.

Because some kids are not comfortable responding during a large group time, encourage boys and girls to ask their parents, small group leaders, or other adults any questions they have about becoming a Christian.

Key passage (5 minutes)

- Key Passage Slide or Poster
- "Celebrate" song

Leader • Has anyone memorized the key passage? Let's hear it!

Invite volunteers to recite the key passage from memory. Then display the key passage slide or poster, and lead the class to say it together.

Leader • Does anyone remember what it means to fear God's name? Yes, it means understanding who He is and that He would be right to punish us for our sin. The prophet Malachi wrote that someone is coming—the sun of righteousness. Who is that? Right, Jesus.

Next, our key passage says that Jesus will come with healing in His wings. That means that when Jesus comes back someday, He will make everything right. The Bible says that when Jesus comes, there will be no more death, crying, or pain. That's worth singing about!

Sing "Celebrate."

Discussion starter video (4 minutes)

Leader • So according to our big picture question and answer, ***Why did Ezra read God's Word? God's Word helped the people obey God so they could be holy.*** The people realized they had sinned, and they were sorry. How do you feel when you realize you've done something wrong? Check out this video.

Show the "Unit 22 Session 3" video.

Leader • When you realize you've done something wrong, you probably feel guilty and sorry. That's how God's people felt. They cried when they realized they had sinned against God.

When we sin, we can repent. That means turning away from our sin and turning back to God. Jesus died for our sin, so when we repent, God forgives our sin.

Sing (3 minutes)

Leader • Before we sing our theme song, can anyone tell me a reason why we praise God? Great answers! We can praise God for many reasons. God gives us His Word— the Bible—so that we can know about Him and His plan

• "Unit 22 Session 3" discussion starter video

• "We Won't Be Shaken" song

to rescue people from sin. Let's praise God together by singing our theme song.

Guide boys and girls to sing "We Won't Be Shaken."

Prayer (2 minutes)

Leader • I've learned so much today. OK, let's practice this climbing technique one more time. Everyone, hold your arms straight up in the air. Now curl your fingers forward like you're grabbing onto some handholds in the rock. Great job! Now before you go, I'm going to pray.

Close in prayer. Pray: "Lord, thank You for giving us Your Word. Thank you for Your law, which shows us Your requirements for holiness. God, we confess that we are lawbreakers. Please forgive us for sinning against You. Thank you for loving us and sending Jesus to die for our sin. Amen."

Dismiss to small groups

The Gospel: God's Plan for Me

Ask kids if they have ever heard the word *gospel*. Clarify that the word *gospel* means "good news." It is the message about Christ, the kingdom of God, and salvation. Use the following guide to share the gospel with kids.

God rules. Explain to kids that the Bible tells us God created everything, and He is in charge of everything. Invite a volunteer to read Genesis 1:1 from the Bible. Read Revelation 4:11 or Colossians 1:16-17 aloud and explain what these verses mean.

We sinned. Tell kids that since the time of Adam and Eve, everyone has chosen to disobey God. (Romans 3:23) The Bible calls this sin. Because God is holy, God cannot be around sin. Sin separates us from God and deserves God's punishment of death. (Romans 6:23)

God provided. Choose a child to read John 3:16 aloud. Say that God sent His Son, Jesus, the perfect solution to our sin problem, to rescue us from the punishment we deserve. It's something we, as sinners, could never earn on our own. Jesus alone saves us. Read and explain Ephesians 2:8-9.

Jesus gives. Share with kids that Jesus lived a perfect life, died on the cross for our sins, and rose again. Because Jesus gave up His life for us, we can be welcomed into God's family for eternity. This is the best gift ever! Read Romans 5:8; 2 Corinthians 5:21; or 1 Peter 3:18.

We respond. Tell kids that they can respond to Jesus. Read Romans 10:9-10,13. Review these aspects of our response: Believe in your heart that Jesus alone saves you through what He's already done on the cross. Repent, turning from self and sin to Jesus. Tell God and others that your faith is in Jesus.

Offer to talk with any child who is interested in responding to Jesus.

Small Group LEADER

Session Title: Ezra Read the Law
Bible Passage: Nehemiah 8:1-12
Big Picture Question: Why did Ezra read God's Word? God's Word helped people obey God so they could be holy.
Key Passage: Malachi 4:2
Unit Christ Connection: God restored a faithful remnant and reminded them of His promise of a new covenant through Jesus Christ.

Key passage activity (5 minutes)

• Key Passage Poster
• paper plates
• marker

Write words or phrases of the key passage and Bible reference on separate paper plates. Hide the plates around the room. Challenge kids to find and collect the hidden plates. Lead them to work together to arrange the plates in the correct order. Guide kids to say the key passage aloud together.

Say • This key passage is the words God spoke through the prophet Malachi. The Book of Malachi is the very last book in the Old Testament. We will learn more about Malachi next time.

Bible story review & Bible skills (10 minutes)

• Bibles, 1 per kid
• Small Group Visual Pack

Option: Retell or review the Bible story using the bolded text of the Bible story script.

Review the timeline from the small group visual pack.

Say • Today's Bible story is from the Book of Nehemiah. Is Nehemiah in the Old Testament or New Testament? (*Old Testament*)

Instruct kids to open their Bibles to Nehemiah 8. Remind them to use the table of contents if they need help.

Assign each kid one verse from Nehemiah 8:1-12. If your group is large, form pairs or small groups. If you have fewer than 12 kids, assign kids more than one verse each.

Instruct each kid to answer the review question for his corresponding verse. There is one question per verse. If a kid needs help finding an answer, ask him to read the verse aloud. Invite the rest of the class to try to identify the correct answer.

1. What did Ezra bring to the people? (*the book of the law of Moses, Neh. 8:1*)
2. Who came to listen to Ezra? (*men, women, and all who were able to understand; Neh. 8:2*)
3. How long did Ezra read? (*from daybreak until noon, about six hours; Neh. 8:3*)
4. Where did Ezra stand? (*on a high wooden platform, Neh. 8:4*)
5. What did the people do when Ezra opened the book of the law? (*stood up, Neh. 8:5*)
6. How did the people worship God? (*with their faces to the ground, Neh. 8:6*)
7. True or False: The Levites explained the law. (*true, Neh. 8:7*)
8. True or False: The Levites tried to confuse people. (*false, Neh. 8:8*)
9. How did the people react when they heard the law? (*They wept, Neh. 8:9*)
10. What made the people strong? (*the joy of the Lord, Neh. 8:10*)
11. What did the Levites say was special about that day? (*It was holy, Neh. 8:11*)
12. Why did the people celebrate? (*They understood the words of the law, Neh. 8:12*)

If you choose to review with boys and girls how to become a Christian, explain that kids are welcome to speak with you or another teacher if they have questions.

- **God rules.** God created and is in charge of everything. (Gen. 1:1; Rev. 4:11; Col. 1:16-17)

- **We sinned.** Since Adam and Eve, everyone has chosen to disobey God. (Rom. 3:23; 6:23)
- **God provided.** God sent His Son, Jesus, to rescue us from the punishment we deserve. (John 3:16; Eph. 2:8-9)
- **Jesus gives.** Jesus lived a perfect life, died on the cross for our sins, and rose again so we can be welcomed into God's family. (Rom. 5:8; 2 Cor. 5:21; 1 Pet. 3:18)
- **We respond.** Believe that Jesus alone saves you. Repent. Tell God that your faith is in Jesus. (Rom. 10:9-10,13)

Activity choice (10 minutes)

Option 1: "Feets" of strength

• small foam ball or beach ball

Guide kids to sit in a circle. Give one player a small foam ball or beach ball to hold between his feet. Kids should pass the ball around the circle using only their feet. The ball may not touch the ground. Count how many times kids can pass the ball without dropping it.

Option: If kids' clothing is not appropriate for passing the ball with their feet, challenge them to participate in one-legged elbow wrestling. Two players stand and interlock their right elbows. Each player uses his left hand to hold his left foot behind him. The first player to drop his foot loses.

Say • You are so strong! You really showed your power. In today's Bible story, we saw how powerful God's Word is. God's Word has the power to change people. The people were happy because even when they forgot about God and sinned against Him, God never forgot about them. God kept His promise to bring them back to their home.

Option 2: A to Z feast

- large sheets of paper, 2
- markers

Form two groups of kids. Give each group a marker and a large sheet of paper. Instruct each group to choose a player to be its scribe. The scribe will list the letters of the alphabet down the side of the paper.

Announce that each team must make a menu of food or drink items for a party. Teams should try to list one item for each letter of the alphabet. After several minutes, call time and encourage kids to share their menus.

Say • After Ezra read from God's Word, the people celebrated. They had a feast! Ezra told them to be happy because God had kept His promise. He brought the people out of exile and back to their land. Even though God's people had forgotten about God and sinned, God did not forget about His people.

Journal and prayer (5 minutes)

- pencils
- journals
- Bibles
- Journal Page, 1 per kid (enhanced CD)
- "Who's Who?" activity page, 1 per kid

Say • *Why did Ezra read God's Word? God's Word helped the people obey God so they could be holy.*

Lead kids to write in their journals about a time they were punished for breaking a rule. How did they feel? Prompt kids to think about how they feel knowing that Jesus died so that their sin could be forgiven.

Say • When Jesus died on the cross, He took the punishment for our sin—all the sins we have committed and even the sins we will commit in the future. When we trust in Jesus as Lord and Savior, our sin is forgiven and we can live for Him.

Invite kids to share prayer requests. Close the group in prayer, or allow a couple volunteers to close the group in prayer. As time allows, lead kids to complete the activity page "Who's Who?"

Leader BIBLE STUDY

After many years living as prisoners in Babylon, God's people had returned to Judah—their promised land. They had worked hard and overcome opposition to rebuild the temple and the walls around Jerusalem. Surely God would restore them … finally! But nothing happened. As they waited, they faced drought and economic uncertainty. God's people probably didn't feel like God had blessed them at all.

"It is useless to serve God," they said. "What have we gained by keeping His requirements?" (Mal. 3:14). Did God still care? It wasn't long until they fell back into the same patterns of sin that led to their exile in the first place: idolatry, covetousness, hypocrisy, arrogance, and abuse of the poor.

But God *did* still love His people. He had been working out His divine plan of redemption, and He never gave up on them. God sent a message to His people through the prophet Malachi.

Malachi was the last of the Old Testament prophets. He spoke to God's people approximately 100 years after the end of the Babylonian captivity. When God's people returned to Judah, the prophets Haggai and Zechariah encouraged them to rebuild the temple. They spoke promises of God's blessing through unity, prosperity, and peace. Malachi's message from God was a wake-up call.

God communicated through Malachi that the people's lack of blessing didn't mean that God didn't care. God exposed His people's sin and made clear that their actions merited punishment. God's people needed to repent and turn back to God. "But for you who fear My name," God said, "the sun of righteousness will rise with healing in its wings" (Mal. 4:2).

Four hundred years of silence followed Malachi's prophecy; God did not communicate to His people. The period brings us to the New Testament, when the silence would be broken by the last prophet before Jesus, John the Baptist. His words about Jesus in John 1:29 offered hope to all who heard: "Here is the Lamb of God, who takes away the sin of the world!"

Older Kids BIBLE STUDY OVERVIEW

Session Title: Malachi the Prophet
Bible Passage: Malachi 1–4
Big Picture Question: Why does God keep His promises? God is faithful, and He loves us.
Key Passage: Malachi 4:2
Unit Christ Connection: God restored a faithful remnant and reminded them of His promise of a new covenant through Jesus Christ.

Small Group Opening

Welcome time ....Page 54
Activity page (5 minutes)..Page 54
Session starter (10 minutes) ....Page 54

Large Group Leader

Countdown ....Page 56
Introduce the session (3 minutes) ....Page 56
Timeline map (1 minute)..Page 56
Big picture question (1 minute) ....Page 57
Tell the Bible story (10 minutes) ....Page 57
The Gospel: God's Plan for Me (optional) ....Page 58
Key passage (5 minutes) ....Page 59
Discussion starter video (4 minutes)...Page 59
Sing (4 minutes)...Page 60
Prayer (2 minutes)...Page 60

Small Group Leader

Key passage activity (5 minutes) ....Page 62
Bible story review & Bible skills (10 minutes)...............................Page 62
Activity choice (10 minutes)...Page 64
Journal and prayer (5 minutes) ....Page 65

The BIBLE STORY

Malachi the Prophet
Malachi 1–4

The Jewish people had returned to the promised land. They had rebuilt the temple and the walls around Jerusalem. **They were ready for God to bless them. The people waited, but nothing happened. Sometimes their lives were hard, and they wondered if God really loved them.** The people became lazy in how they worshiped God.

The Lord loved His people, and He wanted them to be holy. He wanted them to obey Him completely. **So God sent a message to His people through the prophet Malachi** (MAL uh kigh). God gave Malachi a message, and then Malachi told the people what God said. **God's message told the people about their sins and called them to turn back to Him.**

The priests had been disobedient. They were supposed to lead the people in worship, but instead of offering God the best animal sacrifices, the priests offered animals that were stolen, lame, or sick. God said, "I'm not pleased. I will not accept your offerings."

God also **said to the priests, "It is your job to help people follow Me; they look to you for instruction. But you have turned them away from Me.** The things you taught them were wrong."

God gave a warning through Malachi. **He told the people that a day of judgment is coming when God**—the Judge of all the earth—**will punish sin and reward righteousness. God said, "I am going to send My messenger, and he will clear the way before Me."**

The messenger God was going to send would have a very important job: to announce that another messenger was coming and to get the people ready. The coming Messenger—called the Messenger of the covenant—**would be God's promised Messiah.**

Next, God talked about some of the wrong things the people were doing. "You are robbing Me!" God said.

The people were not offering to God a share of their wealth. They had forgotten that everything they had was a gift from God. So God gave them a challenge. "Bring a tenth of your wealth to Me," God said. "And test Me! See if I will not give you even more blessings—more than you can count!"

Some of the people were saying things about God that weren't true. "It is useless to serve God," the people said. "What good is it to serve God? People who live however they want to are better off than we are."

But other people did honor God, and God noticed them. "They will be Mine," God said. "I will have compassion on them."

God said the people would see the difference between those who are righteous and those who are wicked. They would see that it is not useless to serve God, and people who do not serve God are not better off.

"A day is coming," God said, "when everyone who is wicked will be destroyed. But those who honor Me will go out and playfully jump like calves."

Malachi's message from God told the people to be patient. God had not forgotten about them. Life wasn't easy, but if they served God and followed Him, they would be happy on the day when God would keep His promise to rescue His people.

Christ Connection: Malachi was a messenger—a prophet—who told God's people to repent. Malachi also told about another messenger God would send. This messenger, John the Baptist, would call people to repent and get them ready for a final Messenger, Jesus Christ. Jesus would bring good news of salvation.

Small Group OPENING

Session Title: Malachi the Prophet
Bible Passage: Malachi 1–4
Big Picture Question: Why does God keep His promises? God is faithful, and He loves us.
Key Passage: Malachi 4:2
Unit Christ Connection: God restored a faithful remnant and reminded them of His promise of a new covenant through Jesus Christ.

Welcome time

Greet each kid as he or she arrives. Use this time to collect the offering, fill out attendance sheets, and help new kids connect to your group. Invite kids to share about times they have had to wait in line for something. Ask kids if they are patient or impatient when they have to wait.

Activity page (5 minutes)

- "Coming Soon" activity page, 1 per kid
- crayons, markers, or colored pencils

Provide crayons, markers, or colored pencils for kids to use with the "Coming Soon" activity page. Invite each kid to design a billboard to advertise an upcoming holiday, birthday, vacation, or other special event.

After a few minutes, ask volunteers to share their advertisements with the group.

Say • The last book in the Old Testament is the Book of Malachi. Malachi's message from God was about something that was coming relatively soon, about 400 years later.

Session starter (10 minutes)

Option 1: Turn back

- masking tape or painter's tape

Clear an area for kids to play a movement game safely.

Mark a tape line at one side of the room. Guide kids to stand on the tape line. Stand on the other side of the room and explain the rules. During each turn, kids may each choose to take one step or two steps toward you. Then you will call out, "Ones, turn back!" Any kid who took only one step must move back to the start line. Allow kids to step again—one or two steps. If you call, "Twos, turn back!" any kid who took two steps must return to the start. Play several rounds, randomly calling ones or twos to turn back.

Say • Today's Bible story is about God's people in Judah. God sent a prophet named Malachi to talk to His people. Malachi told them to turn back to God.

Option 2: Worth the wait?

• masking tape or painter's tape

Mark a tape line down the center of the room. Instruct kids to stand on either side of the line. You will state a scenario, and each kid must decide if the scenario is something worth waiting on. Players who are willing to wait should stand single file on the tape line. After each scenario, guide all the players to return to the side.

- Your mom puts a fresh batch of cookies in the oven. They won't be ready for 15 minutes.
- A new video game comes out tomorrow. You can be the first to buy it if you stand in line for 7 hours.
- You want to know how your favorite TV show ends, but it is interrupted by a commercial break.
- Your family goes to a new restaurant for dinner, but a table won't be available for 40 minutes.

Say • In today's Bible story, God's people were waiting for God to keep His promises. Did they think it was worth the wait? We'll find out.

Transition to large group

Large Group LEADER

Session Title: Malachi the Prophet
Bible Passage: Malachi 1–4
Big Picture Question: Why does God keep His promises? God is faithful, and He loves us.
Key Passage: Malachi 4:2
Unit Christ Connection: God restored a faithful remnant and reminded them of His promise of a new covenant through Jesus Christ.

Countdown

• countdown video

Show the countdown video as your kids arrive, and set it to end as large group time begins.

Introduce the session (3 minutes)

• umbrella

[Large Group Leader enters carrying an umbrella.]

Leader • Hello again, climbers! I'm [*your name*]. As you can see by this umbrella, I have some bad news about our climbing today. The weather forecasters are reporting a good chance of thunderstorms any time now. Unfortunately, climbing isn't safe in the rain. The rocks get slippery, and you could get struck by lightning.

On the bright side, this is kind of perfect. Here we are under a thunderstorm warning, and today's Bible story is about warnings! You see, God's people didn't understand God's plans, and they started to believe things about God that weren't true. So God sent a prophet to warn them.

Timeline map (1 minute)

• Timeline Map

Use the timeline map to review "Nehemiah Heard News of Jerusalem," "Jerusalem's Walls Rebuilt," and "Ezra Read the Law." Point to each picture as you review.

Leader •Nehemiah heard bad news. He was sad because he found out that his friends and family members were living in a city without walls. Walls were very important because they kept the people safe from their enemies. So Nehemiah got permission from the king of Persia to go to Jerusalem and help his people.

Nehemiah led God's people to work together to rebuild the walls. They finished the walls in 52 days, and then the people were safe from their enemies.

Then, God's people gathered to hear Ezra the priest read God's law. The law in God's Word helped people obey God so they could be holy.

God's people thought their lives would be better than they were. They started to wonder if they should serve God at all. They didn't trust God to keep His promises, but God always keeps His promises.

Big picture question (1 minute)

Leader •That leads me to our big picture question. Our big picture question is, ***Why does God keep His promises?*** That's a good question. I'm not very good at keeping my promises, at least not all of them. Why doesn't God change His mind after He promises something? Does anyone have any ideas? [*Choose a couple volunteers to respond.*] Good guesses. Let's listen to the Bible story to find out.

Tell the Bible story (10 minutes)

- "Malachi the Prophet" video
- Bibles
- Bible Story Picture Slide or Poster
- Big Picture Question Slide or Poster

Open your Bible to Malachi 1 and tell the Bible story in your own words, or show the Bible story video "Malachi the Prophet."

Leader •God sent Malachi to talk to His people. The people knew God had promised to bless them. They waited, but when nothing happened, they started to doubt. They even started to believe things about God that weren't true, like that God didn't love them and that serving Him was a waste of time.

That wasn't true! God did love His people, and serving Him was worth it! Malachi came to warn the people to turn back to God. God had a great plan for them!

Malachi told the people what they were doing wrong. The priests had not been leading the people well. God also said the people were stealing from Him; they didn't want to give God their wealth, but everything they had was actually a gift from God. God didn't ask for all of it, just one-tenth. God wanted them to trust Him with everything. God had promised to bless His people, and God always keeps His promises.

Malachi also said that a messenger was coming. This messenger would get people ready for a greater messenger—the promised Messiah.

Our big picture question is, ***Why does God keep His promises? God is faithful, and He loves us.*** Say the big picture question and answer with me. ***Why does God keep His promises? God is faithful, and He loves us.***

God sent Malachi to remind the people that God is faithful, and He loves them. He loves us too, and He gave us His best—His own Son. God kept His promise to send the Messiah, Jesus, to die for our sins on the cross.

The Gospel: God's Plan for Me (optional)

Using Scripture and the guide provided, explain to boys and girls how to become a Christian. Tell kids how they can respond, and provide counselors to speak with each kid individually. Guide counselors to use open-ended questions to allow kids to determine the direction of the conversation.

Encourage boys and girls to ask their parents, small group leaders, or other adults any questions they have about becoming a Christian.

Key passage (5 minutes)

- Key Passage Slide or Poster
- "Celebrate" song

Leader • Does anyone remember our key passage? It comes from the Book of Malachi. Let's say it together. Lead kids to say the key passage from memory. Then display the key passage poster.

Leader • The last part of the verse says that God's people will go out and jump like calves from the stall. That sounds kind of funny, but leaping calves is what Malachi wanted people to picture when they think about how happy God's people will be. When a calf is kept in a stall, it has enough room to stand and eat and lay down but no room to walk or run. Imagine being stuck inside somewhere for a long time. When you finally get to go outside, you want to run and jump in the air! You are so happy to be free!

The prophet Malachi said that one day God will make all things right. People who are evil will be punished, and people who fear God will leap for joy! That makes me want to sing!

Sing the key passage song "Celebrate."

Discussion starter video (4 minutes)

- "Unit 22 Session 4" discussion starter video

Leader • Malachi warned the people to turn back to God. I wonder if the people listened to Malachi or ignored his warnings. Warnings are important! Check out this video. Show the "Unit 22 Session 4" video.

Leader • Warnings help us know what risks and dangers are ahead. They help us know what to do to keep safe. What are some warnings you have heard or seen lately?

Are you ever tempted to ignore a warning?
Invite kids to share their answers.

Sing (4 minutes)

• "We Won't Be Shaken" song

Leader • Say the big picture question and answer with me. *Why does God keep His promises? God is faithful, and He loves us.* Isn't that wonderful? We never have to worry if God will be true to His word. He always keeps His promises because He is faithful, and He loves us! I don't know about you, but that makes me want to praise Him. Will you sing with me?

Lead boys and girls to sing "We Won't Be Shaken."

Prayer (2 minutes)

Leader • Well, everyone, we didn't technically get off the ground to do any rock climbing, but I have to admit that I am kind of relieved! Oh, I didn't tell you? I am very afraid of heights! But I had so much fun learning about God's people rebuilding Jerusalem's walls, Ezra reading the law, and the prophet Malachi warning God's people. I'm going to pray, and then you can go to your small groups.

Close in prayer.

Dismiss to small groups

The Gospel: God's Plan for Me

Ask kids if they have ever heard the word *gospel*. Clarify that the word *gospel* means "good news." It is the message about Christ, the kingdom of God, and salvation. Use the following guide to share the gospel with kids.

God rules. Explain to kids that the Bible tells us God created everything, and He is in charge of everything. Invite a volunteer to read Genesis 1:1 from the Bible. Read Revelation 4:11 or Colossians 1:16-17 aloud and explain what these verses mean.

We sinned. Tell kids that since the time of Adam and Eve, everyone has chosen to disobey God. (Romans 3:23) The Bible calls this sin. Because God is holy, God cannot be around sin. Sin separates us from God and deserves God's punishment of death. (Romans 6:23)

God provided. Choose a child to read John 3:16 aloud. Say that God sent His Son, Jesus, the perfect solution to our sin problem, to rescue us from the punishment we deserve. It's something we, as sinners, could never earn on our own. Jesus alone saves us. Read and explain Ephesians 2:8-9.

Jesus gives. Share with kids that Jesus lived a perfect life, died on the cross for our sins, and rose again. Because Jesus gave up His life for us, we can be welcomed into God's family for eternity. This is the best gift ever! Read Romans 5:8; 2 Corinthians 5:21; or 1 Peter 3:18.

We respond. Tell kids that they can respond to Jesus. Read Romans 10:9-10,13. Review these aspects of our response: Believe in your heart that Jesus alone saves you through what He's already done on the cross. Repent, turning from self and sin to Jesus. Tell God and others that your faith is in Jesus.

Offer to talk with any child who is interested in responding to Jesus.

Small Group LEADER

Session Title: Malachi the Prophet
Bible Passage: Malachi 1–4
Big Picture Question: Why does God keep His promises? God is faithful, and He loves us.
Key Passage: Malachi 4:2
Unit Christ Connection: God restored a faithful remnant and reminded them of His promise of a new covenant through Jesus Christ.

Key passage activity (5 minutes)

- Key Passage Poster
- colored dot labels, 5 per kid

Give each kid five colored dot labels. Demonstrate how the kids should position their labels on the floor. Arrange four of the dots in a square, shoulder-width apart. Place the fifth dot in the center of the square.

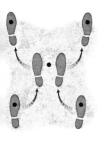

Instruct each kid stand on two of the corner dots. She should say the first word of the key passage, then hop to the center dot with both feet. She will say the next word, and then hop to the second set of dots, one foot on each dot. Then she can turn around and return, saying a word of the verse each time she hops forward.

Allow time for kids to recite the verse several times.

Say • What a wonderful key passage! This is a promise God made, and we know God always keeps His promises. Say it with me: ***Why does God keep His promises? God is faithful, and He loves us.***

Bible story review & Bible skills (10 minutes)

- Bibles, 1 per kid
- Small Group Visual Pack
- sticky notes, 3
- marker

Retell or review the Bible story in your own words, or use the bolded text of the Bible story script.

Form three groups of kids. Write the following references on separate sticky notes and distribute one to each group: *Malachi 3:1*; *Malachi 3:8*; *Malachi 3:10*. Help kids find their groups' assigned verse in their Bibles. Explain that you will ask a review question, and the group that thinks it has the answer should stand. Choose one kid from the standing group to read the verse that answers the review question.

1. Whom did God say He would send to clear or prepare the way before Him? (*His messenger, Mal. 3:1*)
2. What did God say the people were doing wrong? (*robbing Him, Mal. 3:8*)
3. How much did God tell to people to give? (*one-tenth, Mal. 3:10*)

Say • Great job! God promised to bless His people if they would just trust Him. We know that God always keeps His promises. ***Why does God keep His promises? God is faithful, and He loves us.***

• Did you know the Book of Malachi is the last book in the Old Testament? After Malachi's warning, God was quiet. The people did not hear from God for 400 years! Can you imagine waiting that long? But God hadn't forgotten His people. He was getting ready to keep His best promise ever. God would send His Son, Jesus, into the world to save people from their sin.

If you choose to review with boys and girls how to become a Christian, explain that kids are welcome to speak with you or another teacher if they have questions.

• **God rules.** God created and is in charge of everything. (Gen. 1:1; Rev. 4:11; Col. 1:16-17)
• **We sinned.** Since Adam and Eve, everyone has chosen to disobey God. (Rom. 3:23; 6:23)
• **God provided.** God sent His Son, Jesus, to rescue us from the punishment we deserve. (John 3:16; Eph. 2:8-9)

- **Jesus gives.** Jesus lived a perfect life, died on the cross for our sins, and rose again so we can be welcomed into God's family. (Rom. 5:8; 2 Cor. 5:21; 1 Pet. 3:18)
- **We respond.** Believe that Jesus alone saves you. Repent. Tell God that your faith is in Jesus. (Rom. 10:9-10,13)

Activity choice (10 minutes)

Option 1: Pop-up opposites game

- craft sticks
- marker

Write the following words on separate craft sticks and distribute them to the kids: *happy*, *good*, *obey*, *day*, *turn away*, *blessing*, *true*, *remember*. Each kid needs at least one stick. If you need more sticks, make more word sets.

Guide kids to sit in a circle. Explain that kids should pat their legs twice, clap their hands twice, pat their legs twice again, and then clap their hands once. Then kids will pause, and you will announce a word. Lead kids to repeat the rhythm. When you announce a word, kids should read their craft sticks. Whoever has the word's opposite should "pop up," or stand, and shout his word. Kids will repeat the rhythm again, and you will call a new word.

Call out the following words, one at a time, and wait for kids to pop up: sad (*happy*), evil (*good*), disobey (*obey*), night (*day*), turn toward (*turn away*), curse (*blessing*), false (*true*), forget (*remember*).

Say
- Part of Malachi's message from God was about a coming day that will be a terrible day for people who do evil and a happy day for people who honor God.
- People who trust in Jesus as Lord and Savior will be safe, and that will be a happy day when Jesus makes everything right. We can tell others about Jesus so they will be ready on the day of the Lord.

Option 2: Gospel review

- Gospel Plan Poster (enhanced CD)
- paper
- markers or crayons

Provide markers, crayons, and a piece of paper for each kid. Demonstrate how to fold the paper into thirds to make a brochure. Provide a copy of the gospel plan poster for each kid and instruct kids to copy the plan and verse references onto their papers to design a brochure.

Guide kids to look up some of the verses in the Bible. Encourage them to draw pictures on the panels for each part of the gospel plan. As kids work, offer to talk with any child who is interested in responding to Jesus.

Say • God wanted His people to honor Him while they waited. God had not forgotten about them. God had a plan to keep His promise, and He did 400 years later when He sent Jesus to earth.

• God offers us salvation through His Son, Jesus. When we trust in Jesus, He will rescue us from sin.

Journal and prayer (5 minutes)

- pencils
- journals
- Bibles
- Journal Page, 1 per kid (enhanced CD)
- "Leaping Letters" activity page, 1 per kid

Encourage each kid to draw a picture or write a prayer to God in her journal about how she feels knowing that God always keeps His promises.

Say • *Why does God keep His promises? God is faithful, and He loves us.*

Invite kids to share prayer requests. Close the group in prayer, or allow a couple volunteers to close the group in prayer. Thank God for remembering His people and promising to rescue us.

As time allows, lead kids to complete the activity page "Leaping Letters."

Leader BIBLE STUDY

The prophecies concerning Jesus' birth are numerous, and many of them refer to Jesus' lineage. Old Testament prophecies tell of the promised Messiah being born from the seed of a woman (Gen. 3:15); from the seeds of Abraham (Gen. 22:18), Isaac (Gen. 21:12), and Jacob (Num. 24:17); from the tribe of Judah (Micah 5:2); from the line of Jesse (Isa. 11:1); and from the house of David (Jer. 23:5). The prophecies said He would be born of a virgin (Isa. 7:14) and would be the Son of God (1 Chr. 17:13-14; Ps. 2:7). Jesus fulfilled all of these prophecies.

In Bible times, Jews took great care to accurately record family genealogies. The family a person belonged to was directly linked to property rights. Matthew 1:1-17 and Luke 3:23-38 both chronicle the genealogy of Jesus. The account in Matthew presents Jesus as the king of the Jews—the legal heir to the throne of David. The account in Luke was written to Greek Christians and focuses on Jesus' descent from Adam.

Jesus was born as a baby in Bethlehem. He had earthly parents, Mary and Joseph, but His true Father is God. Jesus is fully God and fully man.

As fully God, in Him "the entire fullness of God's nature dwells bodily" (Col. 2:9). As fully man, Jesus has a human body, human mind, and human emotions. (See Luke 2:7,52; Matt. 26:38.) He is our sinless representative (2 Cor. 5:21), sympathetic high priest (Heb. 4:15), and substitute sacrifice (1 John 4:10).

Use this Bible story with the kids you teach to review Jesus' ancestors and their stories in the Old Testament. Help kids recognize that God had been working out His plan to send Jesus over hundreds of years—through Adam, Noah, Abraham, Isaac, Jacob, Jesse, David, Solomon, and Josiah. God sent Jesus to earth to save people from their sins.

Older Kids BIBLE STUDY OVERVIEW

Session Title: Genealogy of Christ

Bible Passage: Matthew 1:1-17; Luke 3:23-38

Big Picture Question: How is Jesus different from any other man? Jesus is fully God and fully man.

Key Passage: Luke 1:76-77

Unit Christ Connection: As prophesied in Isaiah 40:3 and Malachi 3:1, John the Baptist prepared the people for the coming Messiah.

Small Group Opening

Welcome time ....Page 70

Activity page (5 minutes)..Page 70

Session starter (10 minutes) ....Page 70

Large Group Leader

Countdown...Page 72

Introduce the session (3 minutes) ....Page 72

Timeline map (1 minute)..Page 73

Big picture question (1 minute) ....Page 74

Tell the Bible story (10 minutes) ....Page 74

The Gospel: God's Plan for Me (optional) ....Page 75

Key passage (5 minutes) ....Page 75

Discussion starter video (4 minutes)...Page 76

Sing (4 minutes)...Page 76

Prayer (2 minutes)..Page 76

Small Group Leader

Key passage activity (5 minutes) ....Page 78

Bible story review & Bible skills (10 minutes)..............................Page 78

Activity choice (10 minutes)..Page 80

Journal and prayer (5 minutes) ....Page 81

The BIBLE STORY

Genealogy of Christ
Matthew 1:1-17; Luke 3:23-38

Jesus is the Son of God, which means that He is fully God. But when Jesus was born on earth as a little baby, He had human parents too. Their names were Mary and Joseph. Jesus is fully human, too. **Jesus is both fully God and fully human; that makes Him different from any other man.**

Like all people on earth, Jesus' family had a history—a family tree. **Jesus had parents, grandparents, great-grandparents, great-great-grandparents … all the way back to Adam and Eve in the garden of Eden.**

The Bible says Adam and Eve had children. Three of their sons were named Cain, Abel, and Seth. When Seth got older and had a family, his wife had a baby. **Seth named his son Enos** (EE nahs). Enos grew up and had a family too, **and his great-great-grandson was named Enoch** (EE nuhk). Enoch loved God, and he was part of Jesus' family.

Then there was Noah! Noah obeyed God and built an ark to save his family from a great flood. **Noah was part of Jesus' family too. Abraham was in Jesus' family, and so was his son Isaac. When Isaac had a family, one of his sons was named Jacob.** Jacob was part of Jesus' family.

Years later, a man named Salmon (SAL mahn) **was born into Jesus' family** tree. **He married Rahab** (RAY hab), who had hid the Israelite spies when they came to Jericho. **Rahab had a baby, and his name was Boaz** (BOH az). **Boaz** was a farmer, and he **married Ruth. Boaz and Ruth had a son named Obed** (OH bed).

Obed's son was Jesse. Jesse had many sons, and the youngest was David. David was just a boy when he was chosen to be Israel's king. King David liked to write. He wrote songs—called psalms—and some of them were about the time when Jesus would come to earth.

Other people in Jesus' family were kings too. David's son Solomon was a king. King Jehoshaphat (jih HAHSH uh fat) was part of Jesus' family, and so was Uzziah (uh ZIGH uh), Ahaz (AY haz), Hezekiah (HEZ ih kigh uh), and Josiah.

Then came Matthan (MAT than). Matthan's son was named Jacob, and Jacob's son was named Joseph. Joseph is the man who took Mary to be his wife. Mary and Joseph were the earthly parents of Jesus, God's Son—the Messiah.

Christ Connection: Jesus came to earth as a baby in Bethlehem. Jesus had earthly parents, Mary and Joseph, but His true Father is God. Jesus was still God the Son when He came to earth, but He also took on the form of a man. Jesus was born to save people from their sins.

Small Group OPENING

Session Title: Genealogy of Christ
Bible Passage: Matthew 1:1-17; Luke 3:23-38
Big Picture Question: How is Jesus different from any other man? Jesus is fully God and fully man.
Key Passage: Luke 1:76-77
Unit Christ Connection: As prophesied in Isaiah 40:3 and Malachi 3:1, John the Baptist prepared the people for the coming Messiah.

Welcome time

Greet each kid as he or she arrives. Use this time to collect the offering, fill out attendance sheets, and help new kids connect to your group. Ask kids to share how many people are in their families.

Activity page (5 minutes)

- "My Family Tree" activity page, 1 per kid
- pencils

Help kids record the names of their immediate family members on the activity page "My Family Tree." Invite kids to draw pictures of themselves, their parents, and their grandparents. If a kid does not know a relative's first name, suggest he ask his parents at home. Explain that all the people above you on your family tree are your *ancestors*.

Say • Everyone has a family tree—even Jesus. The Bible tells us about Jesus' ancestors: His parents, Mary and Joseph, all the way back to King David, Isaac, Abraham, Noah, and Adam!

- index cards
- pencils

Session starter (10 minutes)

Option 1: Careful copies
Write the following sentence on an index card: *Bring 40 sandwiches to 638 Main St. at 12 p.m.*

Direct kids to sit in a circle. Kids should turn to their left to sit sideways, facing another kid's back. Give each kid a blank index card and a pencil. Give the first player the prepared message. She should copy the message onto her card and pass her card to the player in front of her. Kids will take turns copying the message onto their own cards and then passing their cards around the circle until the message reaches the final player.

Ask the last player to copy the message and then read it aloud. If kids have copied the message accurately, congratulate them on their careful work. If the message contains an error, point out how copying records accurately can be difficult.

Say • During Bible times, copying records accurately was very important. People kept track of who was in their families. The records proved who owned certain areas of land. Today we will look at some family records that show us who was part of Jesus' family.

Option 2: Jesus adjectives

• large pieces of paper, 1 per group
• markers

Form two or three groups of kids. Give each group markers and a large piece of paper. Kids will make a list of words that describe Jesus. Prompt kids to describe things they know to be true about Jesus. Allow several minutes for groups to work, and then invite them to share their lists. If necessary, gently correct any misconceptions about Jesus.

Say • Nice work, everyone. Those words you listed describe Jesus. Did anyone write down the word *human*? Jesus is God the Son, but did you know He came to earth and is both fully God and fully man? We will learn more about that today.

Transition to large group

Large Group LEADER

Session Title: Genealogy of Christ
Bible Passage: Matthew 1:1-17; Luke 3:23-38
Big Picture Question: How is Jesus different from any other man? Jesus is fully God and fully man.
Key Passage: Luke 1:76-77
Unit Christ Connection: As prophesied in Isaiah 40:3 and Malachi 3:1, John the Baptist prepared the people for the coming Messiah.

• room decorations

Tip: Select decorations that fit your ministry and budget.

Suggested Theme Decorating Ideas: Decorate for a birthday party! Make a *Happy Birthday* banner, hang balloons and streamers around the room, and cut triangles to hang from string as a birthday pennant banner. Consider covering some empty boxes with gift wrap and positioning the presents at one side of the large group area. If you wish, invite kids to help you decorate.

Countdown

• countdown video

Show the countdown video as your kids arrive, and set it to end as large group time begins.

Introduce the session (3 minutes)

• crepe paper streamer
• party invitations

[Large Group Leader enters wearing a crepe paper streamer as a scarf and carrying a stack of invitations.]
Leader • Hi, everyone! My name is [*your name*], party planner extraordinaire. How are you? Are you here for the birthday party? Well, the party isn't today; I've just started planning. As a party planner, I have a very important job. I … well, I plan the party. Would you like to help me? I have a few decorations up already. What do you think, should we add more decorations? [*Invite a few kids to help arrange streamers or balloons.*]

I just have to tell you that I love birthday parties! Your birthday is the one special day every year that people get together and celebrate you! On my birthday, my whole family gets together to eat cake and ice cream.

Speaking of family, do you know how many people are in Jesus' family? A lot. More than just His parents, Mary and Joseph. In today's Bible story, we are going to hear about Jesus' ancestors. *Ancestors* are people in your family who came before you, like your great-grandparents, great-great-grandparents, great-great-great grandparents, great-great-great-great … well, you get the idea. Jesus' family goes way back to Adam and Eve.

Timeline map (1 minute)

• Timeline Map

Use the timeline map to briefly review key Old Testament stories. Remember to point to each story on the timeline as you talk about it.

Leader • The Bible stories we have heard so far have been from the Old Testament. The Old Testament tells us the history of the Jewish people. We learned about God creating the world and sin entering the world when Adam and Eve disobeyed God. God promised to bless the world through Abraham's offspring, and then God rescued the Israelites from slavery in Egypt. We learned all about the Israelites being ruled by judges and kings. Sometimes they obeyed God, and a lot of the time they disobeyed God. God sent prophets to warn the people, and He punished the people by sending them into exile. Then God brought His people back to their land.

God had a plan to save His people from the curse of sin. He promised to send a Messiah. God planned for His Son, Jesus, to be part of a Jewish family, and today we will learn about Jesus' earthly family.

Big picture question (1 minute)

Leader • That leads me to our big picture question. Our big picture question is, ***How is Jesus different from any other man?*** Hmm. I know that everyone is different. People have different hair colors and eye colors and heights and weights and hobbies … but something about Jesus makes Him different from anyone else. Let's hear our Bible story to find out.

Tell the Bible story (10 minutes)

- "Genealogy of Christ" video
- Bibles, 1 per kid
- Bible Story Picture Slide or Poster
- Big Picture Question Slide or Poster

Tip: A Bible story script is provided at the beginning of every session. You may use it as you prepare to teach the Bible story in your own words. For a shorter version of the Bible story, read only the bolded text.

Open your Bible to Matthew 1:1-17 and Luke 3:23-38 and tell the Bible story in your own words, or show the Bible story video "Genealogy of Christ."

Leader • You probably know the story of Jesus' birth. God chose Mary and Joseph to be Jesus' parents on earth. For many years, God had promised to send a Messiah to save people from sin. When God kept His promise, He sent Jesus to earth as a baby.

Jesus was God's plan to bring salvation to the world, and God had been working out His plan since the beginning. Many prophets told about Jesus' coming. God promised that Jesus would be part of Abraham's family, Isaac's family, Jacob's family, and King David's family.

God kept His promise! The family records of Jesus show that Jesus' family line stretches all the way back to Adam and Eve. Jesus is a part of Noah's family too. Jesus' family tree includes Abraham, Isaac, and Jacob. It includes Jesse, his son David, and David's son Solomon.

The Old Testament prophets also said that Jesus would be the Son of God. Jesus did not use His status as God to make His life on earth easier. Jesus gave up everything He had in heaven, came to earth, and took on the form of a man. Jesus did not stop being God the Son when He came to earth, but He also became human. Jesus is both fully God and fully man. He was born to save people from their sins.

What is our big picture question? *How is Jesus different from any other man? Jesus is fully God and fully man.* Say the big picture question and answer with me. *How is Jesus different from any other man? Jesus is fully God and fully man.*

The Gospel: God's Plan for Me (optional)

Using Scripture and the guide provided, explain to boys and girls how to become a Christian. Tell kids how they can respond, and provide counselors to speak with each kid individually. Guide counselors to use open-ended questions to allow kids to determine the direction of the conversation.

Because some kids are not comfortable responding during a large group time, encourage boys and girls to ask their parents, small group leaders, or other adults any questions they may have about becoming a Christian.

Key passage (5 minutes)

- Key Passage Slide or Poster
- "You Will Be Called" song

Leader • Our key passage is from the Book of Luke. Let's read it together.

Lead girls and boys to read Luke 1:76-77 aloud. Explain that these verses are about someone God said would come before Jesus, someone who would get people ready for Jesus. Can kids guess who?

Leader • Yes, it's John the Baptist. We will learn more about him soon. Let's practice saying the key passage so we can memorize it.

Read the key passage one line at a time, pausing for kids to echo each line. Invite kids to sing "You Will Be Called."

• "Unit 23 Session 1"
discussion starter
video

Discussion starter video (4 minutes)

Leader • Jesus' Father is God, and He had an earthly family too. Jesus' earthly family goes all the way back to Adam and Eve. Have you ever thought about all of your ancestors who lived before you? Check out this video.

Show the "Unit 23 Session 1" video.

Leader • Everyone has a family tree. Who is the oldest relative you know? Maybe you've met your great-grandparents. Have you ever heard stories about your great-great-grandparents? Or great-great-great-grandparents?

Sing (4 minutes)

• "Ready or Not" song

Leader • Are you ready to sing praises to God? Everybody, stand up as we praise God for sending Jesus to earth. Before we start, *How is Jesus different from any other man? Jesus is fully God and fully man.* That's right! OK, now sing our theme song with me.

Lead boys and girls to sing "Ready or Not."

Prayer (2 minutes)

Leader • I am glad you came to visit me today. Thanks for your help with the decorations. I hope you'll come back next time; I am going to be planning a birthday party menu!

Close in prayer. Thank God for working out His plan to send Jesus from the beginning—through many generations. Thank Him for loving and remembering His people.

Dismiss to small groups

The Gospel: God's Plan for Me

Ask kids if they have ever heard the word *gospel*. Clarify that the word *gospel* means "good news." It is the message about Christ, the kingdom of God, and salvation. Use the following guide to share the gospel with kids.

God rules. Explain to kids that the Bible tells us God created everything, and He is in charge of everything. Invite a volunteer to read Genesis 1:1 from the Bible. Read Revelation 4:11 or Colossians 1:16-17 aloud and explain what these verses mean.

We sinned. Tell kids that since the time of Adam and Eve, everyone has chosen to disobey God. (Romans 3:23) The Bible calls this sin. Because God is holy, God cannot be around sin. Sin separates us from God and deserves God's punishment of death. (Romans 6:23)

God provided. Choose a child to read John 3:16 aloud. Say that God sent His Son, Jesus, the perfect solution to our sin problem, to rescue us from the punishment we deserve. It's something we, as sinners, could never earn on our own. Jesus alone saves us. Read and explain Ephesians 2:8-9.

Jesus gives. Share with kids that Jesus lived a perfect life, died on the cross for our sins, and rose again. Because Jesus gave up His life for us, we can be welcomed into God's family for eternity. This is the best gift ever! Read Romans 5:8; 2 Corinthians 5:21; or 1 Peter 3:18.

We respond. Tell kids that they can respond to Jesus. Read Romans 10:9-10,13. Review these aspects of our response: Believe in your heart that Jesus alone saves you through what He's already done on the cross. Repent, turning from self and sin to Jesus. Tell God and others that your faith is in Jesus.

Offer to talk with any child who is interested in responding to Jesus.

Small Group LEADER

Session Title: Genealogy of Christ
Bible Passage: Matthew 1:1-17; Luke 3:23-38
Big Picture Question: How is Jesus different from any other man? Jesus is fully God and fully man.
Key Passage: Luke 1:76-77
Unit Christ Connection: As prophesied in Isaiah 40:3 and Malachi 3:1, John the Baptist prepared the people for the coming Messiah.

Key passage activity (5 minutes)

• Key Passage Poster

Lead kids to say the key passage together. Then challenge them to recite it in different ways: softly, loudly, quickly, slowly, in a high voice, and in a low voice. Encourage kids to aim for accuracy. As kids learn the verse, hide the key passage poster so they can say the verse from memory.

Say • Zechariah—John the Baptist's father—said these words when John was born. God had a special plan for John's life. John was going to get people ready to meet Jesus.

Bible story review & Bible skills (10 minutes)

• Bibles, 1 per kid
• Small Group Visual Pack

Option: Retell or review the Bible story using the bolded text of the Bible story script.

Say • Our Bible story today comes from the Book of Matthew and the Book of Luke. Are these books in the Old Testament or the New Testament? (*New Testament*) Do you know which Bible division these books are in? (*Gospels*)

Instruct half of the kids to find Matthew 1:1-17 in their Bibles. Direct the other half to find Luke 3:23-38. Help them as needed.

Give kids a minute to look over the names in their assigned passages. Show the timeline from the small group visual pack. Ask review questions about some of the people in Jesus' family with whom kids might be familiar.

Say • Who was the first man God made? (*Adam*)
- Who obeyed God to save his family from a flood? (*Noah*)
- Whom did God test by telling him to sacrifice his son? (*Abraham*)
- Who tricked his father so he could get the blessing his brother deserved? (*Jacob*)
- Who hid the Israelite spies in Jericho? (*Rahab*)
- Which family redeemer married Ruth? (*Boaz*)
- Which king fought Goliath and won? (*David*)
- Which king first built God's temple? (*Solomon*)
- Who were Jesus' parents on earth? (*Joseph, Mary*)
- ***How is Jesus different from any other man? Jesus is fully God and fully man.***

If you choose to review with boys and girls how to become a Christian, explain that kids are welcome to speak with you or another teacher if they have questions.

- **God rules.** God created and is in charge of everything. (Gen. 1:1; Rev. 4:11; Col. 1:16-17)
- **We sinned.** Since Adam and Eve, everyone has chosen to disobey God. (Rom. 3:23; 6:23)
- **God provided.** God sent His Son, Jesus, to rescue us from the punishment we deserve. (John 3:16; Eph. 2:8-9)
- **Jesus gives.** Jesus lived a perfect life, died on the cross for our sins, and rose again so we can be welcomed into God's family. (Rom. 5:8; 2 Cor. 5:21; 1 Pet. 3:18)
- **We respond.** Believe that Jesus alone saves you. Repent. Tell God that your faith is in Jesus. (Rom. 10:9-10,13)

Activity choice (10 minutes)

Option 1: God or man?

• construction paper
• marker

Write the word *God* on one piece of construction paper and the word *man* on another. Post the signs on opposite sides of the room.

Guide kids to stand together in the center of the room. Explain that you will read a statement. Kids should decide if the statement describes something only God can do or if it describes something a man can do. Instruct kids to move quickly to the corresponding sign. If kids are split in their decisions, invite one kid at each sign to explain why he thinks the statement describes that sign.

Say • Jesus was born in Bethlehem. (*man, Matt. 2:1*)
   • Jesus healed people who were sick. (*God, John 4:49-53*)
   • Jesus calmed a storm. (*God, Mark 4:39*)
   • Jesus had brothers and sisters. (*man, Matt. 13:55-56*)
   • Jesus cried when His friend died. (*man, John 11:35*)
   • Jesus got tired, hungry, and thirsty. (*man; John 4:6; Mark 11:12; John 19:28*)
   • Jesus rose from the dead. (*God, Luke 24:6*)

Review the big picture question and answer.

Say • *How is Jesus different from any other man? Jesus is fully God and fully man.*
   • Very good. Jesus came to earth as a baby, and He had earthly parents. But Jesus' true Father is God. Jesus never stopped being God when He came to earth, but He fully took the form of a man. Jesus is fully God and fully man.

• "Timeline Pictures" (enhanced CD)
• masking tape or painter's tape
• marker
• index cards

Option 2: Timeline mix-up

Mark a tape line on the floor, at least 10 feet long. Print the "Timeline Pictures" or write the following names on separate index cards: *Adam, Noah, Abraham, Jacob, Rahab, Boaz and Ruth, King David, King Solomon, Mary and Joseph*. Guide kids to work together to put the pictures in chronological order. As they work, ask them to recall details about each person.

- Adam was the first man God created. (*Gen. 1–2*)
- Noah obeyed God and saved his family from a flood. (*Gen. 6:5–9:17*)
- God tested Abraham and asked him to sacrifice his son. (*Gen. 22:1-19*)
- Jacob tricked his father into giving him a blessing. (*Gen. 25:27-34; 27:1-45*)
- Rahab hid the Israelite spies in Jericho. (*Josh. 2*)
- Boaz married Ruth and took care of her. (*Ruth 1–4*)
- King David fought Goliath and won. (*1 Sam. 16–17*)
- King Solomon first built God's temple. (*1 Kings 6:1–8:66*)
- Mary and Joseph were Jesus' earthly parents. (*Luke 2:1-20*)

Say • Jesus' Father is God, but Jesus had a family on earth too. All of these people are part of Jesus' family! ***How is Jesus different from any other man? Jesus is fully God and fully man.***

Journal and prayer (5 minutes)

- pencils
- journals
- Bibles
- Journal Page, 1 per kid (enhanced CD)
- "Fully, Fully" activity page, 1 per kid

Lead each kid to write or draw on his journal page some ways Jesus showed He is both God and man.

Say • ***How is Jesus different from any other man? Jesus is fully God and fully man.***

Invite kids to share prayer requests. Close the group in prayer or allow a couple volunteers to close the group in prayer. As time allows, lead kids to complete the activity page "Fully, Fully."

Leader BIBLE STUDY

At the end of the Old Testament, God spoke these words to His people: "Look, I am going to send you Elijah the prophet before the great and awesome Day of the Lord comes" (Mal. 4:5). Then a period of silence began. For 400 years, God did not speak to the Jewish people as He had done through the prophets.

The period between the Old and New Testaments was a time of significant change. The Jews saw Persian rule overtaken by Alexander the Great and the Greeks. They were forbidden to practice religion, and the temple in Jerusalem was turned into a pagan shrine. Then Maccabeus, the son of a priest, led the Jewish people to fight for and win their independence, and the temple was cleansed. But the new leaders became corrupt, and the Jews asked a Roman general to restore order.

Rome restored order among the Jews but also submitted them to Roman rule. In 37 B.C., the Roman senate appointed Herod the Great to be king over Palestine—the land of the former kingdoms of Israel and Judah. Herod was king when Jesus was born, and his son Herod Antipas was the Herod whose marriage John the Baptist denounced. (See Matt. 14:3-4.)

Zechariah the priest was serving in the temple during the reign of Herod the Great when Gabriel, an angel of the Lord, appeared. Gabriel said, "Do not be afraid, Zechariah, because your prayer has been heard. Your wife Elizabeth will bear you a son, and you will name him John."

The name *John* means "the Lord is gracious." He certainly is. The foretelling of John's birth by the angel Gabriel marked the coming of the end of God's silence.

Compare Malachi 4:5-6 to Luke 1:16-17. God had big plans for the baby who wasn't even born yet—the baby who would bring joy and delight. God would send John as the last prophet, to prepare the way for the promised Messiah.

Older Kids BIBLE STUDY OVERVIEW

Session Title: John's Birth Was Predicted

Bible Passage: Luke 1:5-25

Big Picture Question: Who announced John's birth? The angel Gabriel told Zechariah that he would have a son.

Key Passage: Luke 1:76-77

Unit Christ Connection: As prophesied in Isaiah 40:3 and Malachi 3:1, John the Baptist prepared the people for the coming Messiah.

Small Group Opening

Welcome time ....Page 86

Activity page (5 minutes)..Page 86

Session starter (10 minutes) ....Page 86

Large Group Leader

Countdown ....Page 88

Introduce the session (3 minutes) ....Page 88

Timeline map (1 minute)..Page 89

Big picture question (1 minute) ....Page 89

Tell the Bible story (10 minutes) ....Page 89

The Gospel: God's Plan for Me (optional) ....Page 90

Key passage (5 minutes) ....Page 90

Discussion starter video (4 minutes)............................Page 91

Sing (4 minutes)...Page 91

Prayer (2 minutes)...Page 92

Small Group Leader

Key passage activity (5 minutes) ....Page 94

Bible story review & Bible skills (10 minutes)..............Page 94

Activity choice (10 minutes)..Page 96

Journal and prayer (5 minutes) ....Page 97

The BIBLE STORY

John's Birth Was Predicted
Luke 1:5-25

Zechariah (ZEK uh RIGH uh) the priest lived in the days when Herod was king of Judea. Zechariah's wife was Elizabeth. Zechariah and Elizabeth both loved God, and they obeyed His laws. But **Zechariah and Elizabeth were getting old, and they did not have any children.**

Zechariah took turns with the other priests serving in God's temple. When it was Zechariah's turn to serve, he went to the temple. Zechariah was chosen to go into the sanctuary and burn incense as an offering to God. Zechariah **went inside the sanctuary**, and a crowd of people stood outside and prayed.

Suddenly Gabriel, an angel of the Lord, appeared to Zechariah. Zechariah was surprised and afraid! But **the angel said, "Don't be afraid, Zechariah, because God has heard your prayer. Your wife Elizabeth will have a son, and you will name him John."**

The angel told Zechariah that many people would be happy about John's birth. He said that God's Spirit would be with John, and God would do great things in John's lifetime. **John would get people ready for the Lord's coming and turn them back to God.** He would lead people who disobey God to change how they were living.

"How can I know that you are telling the truth?" Zechariah asked. "I am an old man, and my wife is getting old too." Was it even possible for Elizabeth to have a baby?

The angel answered, "I am Gabriel, who stands in the presence of God. God sent me to tell you this good news. Now listen! **You will not be able to talk until the day these things happen because you did not believe me.** Everything I said will really happen."

The crowd that had been praying outside started to wonder what was taking Zechariah so long. **When Zechariah finally came out of the sanctuary, he could not speak.** The people realized Zechariah had seen a vision. The only way Zechariah could communicate with the people was by motioning with his hands. When Zechariah finished serving at the temple, he went back home.

After this happened, Zechariah's wife Elizabeth found out she was going to have a baby. She stayed in her house for five months. Elizabeth said, "God has done this for me. He has helped me and has given me a baby."

Christ Connection: God sent John to be the last prophet before Jesus. John would tell people about the coming Savior. John's job was to remind the people what God had said in the past and to get the people ready to meet Jesus.

Small Group OPENING

Session Title: John's Birth Was Predicted
Bible Passage: Luke 1:5-25
Big Picture Question: Who announced John's birth? The angel Gabriel told Zechariah that he would have a son.
Key Passage: Luke 1:76-77
Unit Christ Connection: As prophesied in Isaiah 40:3 and Malachi 3:1, John the Baptist prepared the people for the coming Messiah.

Welcome time

Greet each kid as he or she arrives. Use this time to collect the offering, fill out attendance sheets, and help new kids connect to your group. Ask kids to share the greatest announcements they've ever heard.

Activity page (5 minutes)

- "Get Ready" activity page, 1 per kid
- pencils

Prompt kids to think about all the things they did to get ready for church today. Invite kids to work individually or in pairs to make a list on the "Get Ready" activity page. Then select a couple volunteers to share their routines.

Say • Sometimes God's people needed a little help getting ready. God had a plan to help them get ready.

Session starter (10 minutes)

Option 1: Silent preparations
Invite kids to play a game of charades. Kids will take turns acting out something they do to get ready in the morning. Remind actors that they may not speak while acting. The group should try to guess what the actor is doing.

Kids may choose their own getting ready activities, but be prepared to offer suggestions (brushing teeth, combing hair, feeding a pet, tying shoes, eating breakfast). Ask kids to whisper their own ideas to you before they act them out.

Say • Between the Book of Malachi (the last book in the Old Testament) and the Gospels (the first books in the New Testament) God was silent. He did not speak in this way to His people for 400 years! A lot changed for God's people during that time. The rulers in Rome took over, and some people might have wondered if God forgot about His people. God did not forget. In today's Bible story, we will hear what God said when He finally broke the silence.

Option 2: Party prep relay

• tablecloths, 2
• plates, 2
• cups, 2
• napkins, 2
• cards and envelopes
• deflated balloons
• Allergy Alert
  (enhanced CD)

Form two teams of kids. Guide them to stand single file at one side of the room. Position across from each team a folded tablecloth, several cards and envelopes, several deflated balloons, a plate, a cup, and a napkin.

Explain that kids will race one at a time to their team's supplies. Each kid may choose to complete one of the following tasks to prepare for a party:

• Spread the tablecloth on the floor or a table.
• Put a card into an envelope and seal it.
• Blow up a balloon and tie it.
• Arrange a place setting with a napkin in the center of a plate and the cup to the right of the plate.

The first team to finish preparing should sit down. Congratulate the teams on their hard work.

Say • In today's Bible story, God's people had not heard from God for 400 years, but He told them it was time to get ready.

Transition to large group

Large Group LEADER

Session Title: John's Birth Was Predicted
Bible Passage: Luke 1:5-25
Big Picture Question: Who announced John's birth? The angel Gabriel told Zechariah that he would have a son.
Key Passage: Luke 1:76-77
Unit Christ Connection: As prophesied in Isaiah 40:3 and Malachi 3:1, John the Baptist prepared the people for the coming Messiah.

Countdown

• countdown video

Show the countdown video as your kids arrive, and set it to end as large group time begins.

Introduce the session (3 minutes)

• cookbook
• pencil

[Large Group Leader enters carrying a cookbook and a pencil. Flip through the cookbook before noticing kids.]

Leader • Hello, everyone! You're back! Are you ready to plan a birthday party? You did a great job helping me with decorations last week. Today I need to plan the menu. I'm hoping this cookbook will give me some ideas. What types of food should we serve? Cake? Cookies? Ice cream? Oh, I'm getting a stomachache just thinking about all of that.

In case you forgot, my name is [*your name*], party planner extraordinaire! I really appreciate your help getting ready for this party. That reminds me of today's Bible story. It's about getting ready. It's about a baby God announced—a baby with a big job of getting people ready. That sounds like a lot of responsibility. Don't worry, though. The baby grew up first, and then he helped people get ready!

Timeline map (1 minute)

• Timeline Map

Direct kids' attention to the timeline map and point out "Genealogy of Christ."

Leader • Can anyone tell me whose family we learned about last week? Yes! We learned about Jesus' family. You can find stories about some of the people in Jesus' family throughout the Old Testament. The Old Testament tells the story of the Israelites—God's chosen people— who later became known as Jews because they were from Judah. God promised to send a Messiah from the Jewish people. The New Testament begins with God's keeping of that promise.

Big picture question (1 minute)

Leader • That leads me to our big picture question. Our big picture question is, *Who announced John's birth?* God's people had not heard from God for hundreds of years. Then God spoke a message through someone. I wonder who it was. Listen to today's Bible story to find out.

Tell the Bible story (10 minutes)

• "John's Birth Was Predicted" video
• Bibles, 1 per kid
• Bible Story Picture Slide or Poster
• Big Picture Question Slide or Poster

Open your Bible to Luke 1:5-25 and tell the Bible story in your own words, or show the Bible story video "John's Birth Was Predicted."

Leader • Zechariah and his wife, Elizabeth, were old, and they did not have any children. Zechariah was just doing his job as a priest in the temple when he saw an angel! The angel Gabriel told Zechariah that he and his wife were going to be parents!

That's the answer to our big picture question! *Who announced John's birth? The angel Gabriel told Zechariah that he would have a son.* Say the big picture question and answer with me. *Who announced John's*

***birth? The angel Gabriel told Zechariah that he would
have a son.***

Do you think Zechariah was excited? He probably was!
Then Gabriel told Zechariah to name his son John. Maybe
this news sounded too good to be true! Zechariah wasn't
sure if he could believe the angel. Was Gabriel telling
the truth? Wasn't Elizabeth too old to have a baby? So
Gabriel told Zechariah that he wouldn't be able to talk
until his words came true.

When Zechariah left the temple, he couldn't talk. He
had to gesture with his hands to communicate. Elizabeth
found out she was going to have a baby. She knew the
baby was a gift from God.

God was planning for this baby to be a prophet. God's
people had not heard from God for 400 years, but God
had not forgotten His plan to save people from their
sin. John would grow up and remind people about the
Messiah God had promised to send. John was going to get
people ready to meet Jesus.

The Gospel: God's Plan for Me (optional)

Using Scripture and the guide provided, explain to boys
and girls how to become a Christian. Tell kids how they
can respond, and provide counselors to speak with each kid
individually. Guide counselors to use open-ended questions
to allow kids to determine the direction of the conversation.

Encourage boys and girls to ask their parents, small
group leaders, or other adults any questions they may have
about becoming a Christian.

- Key Passage Slide or
  Poster
- "You Will Be Called"
  song
- sticky notes

Key passage (5 minutes)

Leader • Does anyone remember our key passage from last
week? Let's say it together.

Lead the boys and girls to read the key passage aloud. Explain that God chose John to go before Jesus and prepare the people. The people sinned, and they needed a Savior. John would tell them to repent of their sins. He would tell them to be sorry for disobeying God and that they needed to turn back to Him. John was going to call the people to repent and be baptized.

Use a sticky note to cover up part of the key passage and challenge kids to say it from memory. Cover more of the key passage with additional sticky notes as kids memorize the words. Lead the group to say the key passage several times. Then sing "You Will Be Called."

Discussion starter video (4 minutes)

• "Unit 23 Session 2" discussion starter video

Leader •According to our big picture question and answer, *Who announced John's birth? The angel Gabriel told Zechariah that he would have a son.* God already had a plan for John's life, even before John was born! John would tell people to get ready for Jesus.

What might have happened if John hadn't done his job? Has anything ever happened that you weren't ready for? Check out this video.

Show the "Unit 23 Session 2" video.

Leader •What happens when we aren't ready? Have you ever missed the bus because you weren't ready?

Allow kids to respond. Emphasize that we can miss out on important events when we aren't ready. John's job was to get people ready to meet Jesus so they wouldn't miss out on the good news Jesus had for them.

Sing (4 minutes)

• "Ready or Not" song

Leader •*Who announced John's birth? The angel Gabriel told Zechariah that he would have a son.* Great job. God was working out His plan to send Jesus to earth. He planned for Zechariah's son to help people get ready for Jesus. God works everything out for His glory and our good. Stand with me and let's sing our theme song.

Lead boys and girls to sing "Ready or Not."

Prayer (2 minutes)

Leader • Zechariah and Elizabeth must have been very excited to find out they were going to have a baby! Do you know what that baby could celebrate every year? You guessed it—a birthday! Before you go to your small groups, let's take a vote on what types of food we want to have at a birthday party. If you like cake and ice cream, raise your hand. OK, everyone in favor of fruit, raise your hand. And finally, who prefers pizza for the party? Thank you! I'll finish up this menu in no time.

Will you say the big picture question and answer with me one more time? Then I will close in prayer. *Who announced John's birth? The angel Gabriel told Zechariah that he would have a son.*

Close in prayer.

Dismiss to small groups

The Gospel: God's Plan for Me

Ask kids if they have ever heard the word *gospel*. Clarify that the word *gospel* means "good news." It is the message about Christ, the kingdom of God, and salvation. Use the following guide to share the gospel with kids.

God rules. Explain to kids that the Bible tells us God created everything, and He is in charge of everything. Invite a volunteer to read Genesis 1:1 from the Bible. Read Revelation 4:11 or Colossians 1:16-17 aloud and explain what these verses mean.

We sinned. Tell kids that since the time of Adam and Eve, everyone has chosen to disobey God. (Romans 3:23) The Bible calls this sin. Because God is holy, God cannot be around sin. Sin separates us from God and deserves God's punishment of death. (Romans 6:23)

God provided. Choose a child to read John 3:16 aloud. Say that God sent His Son, Jesus, the perfect solution to our sin problem, to rescue us from the punishment we deserve. It's something we, as sinners, could never earn on our own. Jesus alone saves us. Read and explain Ephesians 2:8-9.

Jesus gives. Share with kids that Jesus lived a perfect life, died on the cross for our sins, and rose again. Because Jesus gave up His life for us, we can be welcomed into God's family for eternity. This is the best gift ever! Read Romans 5:8; 2 Corinthians 5:21; or 1 Peter 3:18.

We respond. Tell kids that they can respond to Jesus. Read Romans 10:9-10,13. Review these aspects of our response: Believe in your heart that Jesus alone saves you through what He's already done on the cross. Repent, turning from self and sin to Jesus. Tell God and others that your faith is in Jesus.

Offer to talk with any child who is interested in responding to Jesus.

Small Group LEADER

Session Title: John's Birth Was Predicted
Bible Passage: Luke 1:5-25
Big Picture Question: Who announced John's birth? The angel Gabriel
 told Zechariah that he would have a son.
Key Passage: Luke 1:76-77
Unit Christ Connection: As prophesied in Isaiah 40:3 and Malachi 3:1,
 John the Baptist prepared the people for the coming Messiah.

Key passage activity (5 minutes)

- Key Passage Poster
- paper plates or index cards
- marker
- tape

Write phrases of the key passage on several paper plates or
index cards. Mix up the plates and tape them securely to the
floor. If your group is large, prepare more than one set.

Challenge kids to take turns jumping from plate to plate
in the correct order as they recite the key passage from
memory. If a kid makes a mistake, guide him to back up
to the previous word and try again. As kids master the key
passage, instruct them to jump faster.

Say • Good job, everyone! This Bible passage tells us
God's plan for John. *Who announced John's birth?*
The angel Gabriel told Zechariah that he would
have a son.

Bible story review & Bible skills (10 minutes)

- Bibles, 1 per kid
- Small Group Visual Pack

Option: Retell or review the Bible story using the bolded text of the Bible story script.

Help kids find Luke 1:5-25 in their Bibles. Invite kids to
take turns reading the passage aloud. Kids may read two or
three verses at a time.

Show the timeline map in the small group visual pack.
Remind kids that after the prophet Malachi, God had not
spoken to His people in 400 years. Zechariah must have
been very surprised to see the angel!

Ask review questions about the Bible story. Allow time for kids to find the answer in the Bible and then choose someone with a raised hand to give the answer. Ask her which verse reveals the answer.

Say • Who was the king when Zechariah worked as a priest? (*Herod, Luke 1:5*)

• What was the name of Zechariah's wife? (*Elizabeth, Luke 1:5*)

• How did Zechariah feel when he saw the angel? (*He was afraid, Luke 1:12*)

• What did the angel tell Zechariah to name his son? (*John, Luke 1:13*)

• What was the angel's name? (*Gabriel, Luke 1:19*)

• What was Zechariah unable to do after he saw the angel? (*speak, Luke 1:20*)

If you choose to review with boys and girls how to become a Christian, explain that kids are welcome to speak with you or another teacher if they have questions.

• **God rules.** God created and is in charge of everything. (Gen. 1:1; Rev. 4:11; Col. 1:16-17)

• **We sinned.** Since Adam and Eve, everyone has chosen to disobey God. (Rom. 3:23; 6:23)

• **God provided.** God sent His Son, Jesus, to rescue us from the punishment we deserve. (John 3:16; Eph. 2:8-9)

• **Jesus gives.** Jesus lived a perfect life, died on the cross for our sins, and rose again so we can be welcomed into God's family. (Rom. 5:8; 2 Cor. 5:21; 1 Pet. 3:18)

• **We respond.** Believe that Jesus alone saves you. Repent. Tell God that your faith is in Jesus. (Rom. 10:9-10,13)

Activity choice (10 minutes)

Option 1: It's a boy!

Form groups of three or four kids. Give each group a large sheet of paper, markers, and other decorating supplies.

- large sheets of paper
- markers
- other decorating supplies

Explain that parents often announce when they are expecting a baby. Invite each group to work together to design a baby announcement for John. Kids should include the baby's name and gender, the parents' names, and some words that describe John. Lead kids to refer to Luke 1:17 for a description of God's plan for John.

Kids may wish to draw a picture of a baby boy and decorate the announcement with other embellishments.

Say •*Who announced John's birth? The angel Gabriel told Zechariah that he would have a son.*

Option 2: Prophet roundup

- balloons, 16
- permanent marker
- masking tape or painter's tape

Use a permanent marker to write the following prophet names on 16 separate balloons: *Isaiah, Jeremiah, Ezekiel, Daniel, Hosea, Joel, Amos, Obadiah, Jonah, Micah, Nahum, Habakkuk, Zephaniah, Haggai, Zechariah, Malachi.* Use tape to mark two large, square outlines in separate areas of the room.

Instruct kids to work together to sort each prophet into his correct Bible division: Major Prophets or Minor Prophets. When kids finish, check their work. The Major Prophets include Isaiah, Jeremiah, Ezekiel, and Daniel. The remaining 12 are the Minor Prophets.

Say •You really know your prophets! In the Old Testament, God sent prophets to talk to His people. The prophets listened to God, and then they told the people what He said. Many of the Old Testament prophets told people that Jesus was coming.

•Zechariah heard great news; he and Elizabeth were

going to be parents! *Who announced John's birth?* *The angel Gabriel told Zechariah that he would have a son.* John would be a prophet, too. He would tell people about Jesus.

If time allows, challenge kids to arrange the balloons in the order they appear in the Bible.

Journal and prayer (5 minutes)

- pencils
- journals
- Bibles
- Journal Page, 1 per kid (enhanced CD)
- "Switcheroo" activity page, 1 per kid

Lead each kid to write in her journal about some news she heard that made her happy. Explain that God's people knew God had promised a Messiah, and they were waiting for news of Him.

Remind kids that God was silent for 400 years during the time between the Old Testament and New Testament. The announcement that John was coming was exciting; it meant that the Messiah was coming soon!

Say • *Who announced John's birth? The angel Gabriel told Zechariah that he would have a son.*

Invite kids to share prayer requests. Close the group in prayer. As time allows, lead kids to complete the activity page "Switcheroo."

Leader BIBLE STUDY

God's people did not hear a clear message from God for hundreds of years. Then one day, Gabriel—an angel of the Lord—told a man that his wife, Elizabeth, was going to have a baby. The baby's name would be John. Then the angel Gabriel appeared to Mary and told her that she would have a baby, and He would be God's Son.

Mary and Elizabeth were relatives. Elizabeth was old and barren; she and her husband, Zechariah, had no children. Mary was a young girl—likely in her early teens. She was a virgin, engaged to be married to Joseph. The announcements of these pregnancies were miraculous for both women. Both babies had been foretold by the prophet Isaiah—John in Isaiah 40:3 and Jesus in Isaiah 7:14.

The angel Gabriel told Mary that Elizabeth was pregnant too, and Mary hurried to see her. The journey would not have been easy. Mary traveled nearly one hundred miles to see Elizabeth, and her arrival brought great joy to both Elizabeth and Elizabeth's unborn baby. In the presence of the unborn Messiah, John leaped in Elizabeth's belly. Elizabeth was filled with the Holy Spirit, and she said, "Mary, you are blessed!"

The story of Mary's visit with Elizabeth gives us a remarkable picture of women living by faith. Being a young, unwed pregnant woman could have caused Mary to worry. Instead, her response is marked by her trust in God. Mary's song reflects her knowledge of God's Word and her understanding of who God is.

Mary worshiped God because the coming of the promised Savior was good news! People had been waiting hundreds of years for the Messiah. "My soul proclaims the greatness of the Lord," Mary sang. Being the mother of Jesus was no small task, but Mary trusted that God was in charge.

The words of Mary's song were a testimony of God's mercy, might, grace, generosity, and faithfulness. Mary knew these things, and that is why she sang.

Older Kids BIBLE STUDY OVERVIEW

Session Title: Mary Visited Elizabeth
Bible Passage: Luke 1:39-56
Big Picture Question: What was special about Mary's baby? Jesus is
   God's Son.
Key Passage: Luke 1:76-77
Unit Christ Connection: As prophesied in Isaiah 40:3 and Malachi 3:1,
   John the Baptist prepared the people for the coming Messiah.

Small Group Opening

Welcome time ....Page 102
Activity page (5 minutes)..Page 102
Session starter (10 minutes) ....Page 102

Large Group Leader

Countdown ....Page 104
Introduce the session (3 minutes) ....Page 104
Timeline map (1 minute)...Page 105
Big picture question (1 minute) ....Page 105
Tell the Bible story (10 minutes) ....Page 105
The Gospel: God's Plan for Me (optional) ....Page 106
Key passage (5 minutes) ....Page 107
Discussion starter video (4 minutes).................................Page 107
Sing (4 minutes)..Page 107
Prayer (2 minutes)..Page 108

Small Group Leader

Key passage activity (5 minutes) ....Page 110
Bible story review & Bible skills (10 minutes)......................Page 110
Activity choice (10 minutes)..Page 112
Journal and prayer (5 minutes) ....Page 113

The BIBLE STORY

Mary Visited Elizabeth
Luke 1:39-56

The angel Gabriel had appeared to Mary and said that Mary was going to have a baby. Gabriel said that the baby would be God's Son! He also told Mary that her relative Elizabeth was going to have a baby too, even though Elizabeth was old.

Mary hurried to the town in Judah **where her relative Elizabeth lived.** When Mary got there, she went into the house and called out to Elizabeth. **When Mary came in the house, Elizabeth's baby leaped in her belly**, and Elizabeth was filled with the Holy Spirit.

Elizabeth said, "You are blessed, Mary! And your baby will be blessed!"

Elizabeth could hardly believe what was happening. These things were so wonderful! "How could the mother of God's Son come to me?" she wondered. **Then Elizabeth said, "As soon as I heard you, Mary, the baby inside me leaped for joy!"** Elizabeth said that Mary would be blessed for believing God's words. Everything God said would happen would really happen.

Mary was so happy. She praised God with a song about how great He is. The song went like this:

> **The Lord is great and my spirit rejoices in Him!**
> **He has looked on me**—His humble servant—**with favor.**
> Surely, from now on, all people will call me blessed because
> God has done great things for me.
> His name is holy.
> He shows mercy to all who have faith in Him—who believe in
> Him without seeing Him.
> With His mighty arm, God has scattered people who are proud.
> He has taken mighty kings off their thrones, and He has given
> the people who are ordinary and poor places of honor.
> He has filled up people who are hungry with good things, and
> He sent the rich people away with nothing.
> **God has helped His servant**—the nation of Israel—**and He**

has remembered the promise He made to Abraham and his descendants.

Mary knew every family in the future would say she was blessed because God was going to do great things for her through Jesus. God was keeping His promise to bless the whole world through Jesus. Mary stayed with Elizabeth about three months, and then she went back to her home in Nazareth.

Christ Connection: God kept His promise to Abraham and his descendants. The coming of the promised Savior was good news! Before Jesus was born, people rejoiced and praised God for His Son. Mary and Elizabeth worshiped God because of Jesus.

Small Group OPENING

Session Title: Mary Visited Elizabeth
Bible Passage: Luke 1:39-56
Big Picture Question: What was special about Mary's baby? Jesus is God's Son.
Key Passage: Luke 1:76-77
Unit Christ Connection: As prophesied in Isaiah 40:3 and Malachi 3:1, John the Baptist prepared the people for the coming Messiah.

Welcome time

Greet each kid as he or she arrives. Use this time to collect the offering, fill out attendance sheets, and help new kids connect to your group.

Invite kids to share the names of cities or states where their relatives live. How often do they visit? How do they get there?

Activity page (5 minutes)

• "Animal Babies" activity page, 1 per kid
• pencils

Challenge kids to complete the "Animal Babies" activity page. They should match each adult animal with the name of its young. Review the answers as a group. (*hatchling, alligator; cub, lion; piglet, pig; fawn, deer; kitten, cat; tadpole, frog; joey, kangaroo; fledgling, owl*)

Say • Today we are going to hear a Bible story about two women. Each of them was going to have a baby.

Session starter (10 minutes)

• sticky notes
• pencils

Option 1: Awesome adjectives
Give each kid a sticky note and a pencil. Explain that an *adjective* is a word that describes a noun (person, place, or thing). Give examples: tall, happy, green, sweet, calm, slow,

and so forth. Instruct each kid to write on his sticky note an adjective that describes a friend. When kids are finished, invite them to attach their sticky notes to a focal wall. Read several of the adjectives aloud.

Say • Many of these adjectives describe special friends. Friends can be special to us when they are kind, funny, understanding, or happy.

• In our Bible story today, we will learn a little about Mary's baby. Mary visited her relative Elizabeth, and Elizabeth told Mary that she was blessed because her baby was very special.

Option 2: Musical matches

• index cards
• marker

Write the names of several musical instruments on separate index cards. Make a set of two or four cards per instrument so you have one card per kid. Consider these suggestions: trumpet, trombone, xylophone, piano, drums, guitar, saxophone, or triangle.

Give each kid an instrument card and instruct kids to not let anyone else see their cards. Each kid should look at his card and then use motions and sounds to act out playing the instrument. Kids will move about the room, trying to find their matches. When all the kids have found their matches, call for everyone to stop "playing" their instruments. Point to each pair or group and allow them to demonstrate their instruments for the class.

Say • Instruments are one of the best ways to make music! How else can we make music? That's right; we can use our voices. Raise your hand if you like to sing. In today's Bible story, Jesus' mother, Mary, worshiped God with a song because she was so happy.

Transition to large group

Large Group LEADER

Session Title: Mary Visited Elizabeth
Bible Passage: Luke 1:39-56
Big Picture Question: What was special about Mary's baby? Jesus is
  God's Son.
Key Passage: Luke 1:76-77
Unit Christ Connection: As prophesied in Isaiah 40:3 and Malachi 3:1,
  John the Baptist prepared the people for the coming Messiah.

Countdown

• countdown video

Show the countdown video as your kids arrive, and set it to
end as large group time begins.

Introduce the session (3 minutes)

• party hat
• clipboard
• pencil

*[Large Group Leader enters wearing a party hat and
carrying a clipboard and pencil.]*

Leader • Hi, everyone! Boy, am I glad to see you. Do
  you know what today is? No, it's not party day. That's
  a good guess, though. Today is week-before-the-party
  day! In case you forgot, I'm [*your name*], party planner
  extraordinaire! Let's see, we have already sent the
  invitations, done the decorations, and ordered the food.
  Now it's time to plan some party games! I hope you
  have some good ideas. Playing games is a great way to
  celebrate a birthday.

  Speaking of celebrating birthdays, today's Bible story
  is about a celebration. Mary and Elizabeth were relatives
  who were both expecting babies. The babies hadn't
  been born yet, but Mary and Elizabeth were already
  celebrating.

Timeline map (1 minute)

• Timeline Map

Remember to point to the Bible stories "Genealogy of Christ" and "John's Birth Is Predicted" on the timeline as you review.

Leader • Let's take a look at our timeline map. Since we've started learning about the New Testament, we heard about Jesus' family. God came from the family of King David, Ruth, Isaac, Abraham, Noah, … all the way back to Adam and Eve. Those people were Jesus' earthly family. Jesus is God's Son. He is fully God and fully man.

Then we learned about another promised baby. After 400 years of silence, God spoke through the angel Gabriel to announce to Zechariah that his wife, Elizabeth, would have a son. Elizabeth was a relative of Mary; each of them was expecting a baby.

Big picture question (1 minute)

Leader • That leads me to our big picture question. Our big picture question is, ***What was special about Mary's baby?*** Every baby is special. God had a special plan for Elizabeth's baby, but there was something extra-special about Mary's baby. Let's listen to the Bible story to find out the answer to our big picture question.

Tell the Bible story (10 minutes)

• "Mary Visited Elizabeth" video
• Bibles, 1 per kid
• Bible Story Picture Slide or Poster
• Big Picture Question Slide or Poster

Open your Bible to Luke 1:39-56 and tell the Bible story in your own words, or show the Bible story video "Mary Visited Elizabeth."

Leader • The angel Gabriel had appeared to Elizabeth's husband, Zechariah, to announce that Elizabeth would have a son named John. Gabriel also appeared to Mary. He told her that she was going to have a son too. Then Mary hurried to see Elizabeth.

What happened when Mary greeted Elizabeth? Even in Elizabeth's belly, John heard Mary's voice and knew that Jesus was there. And he leaped for joy! John had a very special purpose for his life. God had chosen John to be a messenger. John was going to go before Jesus and get people ready for Him. John was a very special baby, but Jesus was even more important than John!

Our big picture question today is, **What was special about Mary's baby? Jesus is God's Son.** Say the big picture question and answer with me. **What was special about Mary's baby? Jesus is God's Son.**

Mary was so happy to visit Elizabeth. Elizabeth confirmed that Mary's baby was a great gift from God. Mary praised God with a song. Mary said that the Lord is great. He had favor on Mary even though she hadn't done anything to deserve His favor. Mary said that people who lived years after her would call her blessed because of the great things God had done for her. Mary also praised God by telling of the things God had done: He had scattered the people who were proud because their thoughts did not honor God. He took kings off their thrones and gave people who were hungry good things to satisfy them. God had helped His people—the people of Israel—even though they didn't deserve His help.

God was keeping the promise He made to Abraham so many years ago. Mary's baby, Jesus, was going to be the offspring of Abraham who would bless all the people in the world.

The Gospel: God's Plan for Me (optional)

Using Scripture and the guide provided, explain to boys and girls how to become a Christian. Tell kids how they can respond, and provide counselors to speak with each kid individually. Guide counselors to use open-ended questions to allow kids to determine the direction of the conversation.

Encourage boys and girls to ask their parents, small group leaders, or other adults any questions they may have about becoming a Christian.

Key passage (5 minutes)

• Key Passage Slide or Poster
• "You Will Be Called" song

Leader • Does anyone have our key passage memorized? Let's read it together.

Lead boys and girls to read the key passage. Cover the key passage poster and challenge them to say it again. Explain that God's plan for John's life was that John would teach people. He would teach them that they could be saved from their sins. He would teach them that Jesus was coming so that they could be forgiven. Sing "You Will Be Called."

Discussion starter video (4 minutes)

• "Unit 23 Session 3" discussion starter video

Leader • According to our big picture question and answer, *What was special about Mary's baby? Jesus is God's Son.* Even though John wasn't born yet, he was happy about Jesus and leaped in Elizabeth's belly. What do you do when you are very happy? Check out this video.

Show the "Unit 23 Session 3" video.

Leader • Mary, Elizabeth, and John were happy about Jesus. Jesus was a good gift from God. Mary praised God with a song.

Prompt kids to demonstrate how they react when they are very happy.

Sing (4 minutes)

• "Ready or Not" song

Leader • John leaped in Elizabeth's belly before he and Jesus were even born. Mary praised God with a song. Jesus is the Messiah God promised! Let's praise Him!

Do I have a few volunteers who want to lead our group to sing our theme song?

Choose a few kids to lead the rest of the group in singing "Ready or Not."

Prayer (2 minutes)

Leader •Thank you all for being here. Before you go to your small groups, does anyone have an idea for a party game we can play next week? [*Choose a few volunteers to make suggestions.*] Oh, those games sound like so much fun! I think all of you could be party planner extraordinaires too!

Close in prayer. Pray: "Lord, thank You for the good gift of babies. Your plans for Jesus and John were perfect. We agree with the words Mary said. You are great, and You do great things. Amen."

Dismiss to small groups

The Gospel: God's Plan for Me

Ask kids if they have ever heard the word *gospel*. Clarify that the word *gospel* means "good news." It is the message about Christ, the kingdom of God, and salvation. Use the following guide to share the gospel with kids.

God rules. Explain to kids that the Bible tells us God created everything, and He is in charge of everything. Invite a volunteer to read Genesis 1:1 from the Bible. Read Revelation 4:11 or Colossians 1:16-17 aloud and explain what these verses mean.

We sinned. Tell kids that since the time of Adam and Eve, everyone has chosen to disobey God. (Romans 3:23) The Bible calls this sin. Because God is holy, God cannot be around sin. Sin separates us from God and deserves God's punishment of death. (Romans 6:23)

God provided. Choose a child to read John 3:16 aloud. Say that God sent His Son, Jesus, the perfect solution to our sin problem, to rescue us from the punishment we deserve. It's something we, as sinners, could never earn on our own. Jesus alone saves us. Read and explain Ephesians 2:8-9.

Jesus gives. Share with kids that Jesus lived a perfect life, died on the cross for our sins, and rose again. Because Jesus gave up His life for us, we can be welcomed into God's family for eternity. This is the best gift ever! Read Romans 5:8; 2 Corinthians 5:21; or 1 Peter 3:18.

We respond. Tell kids that they can respond to Jesus. Read Romans 10:9-10,13. Review these aspects of our response: Believe in your heart that Jesus alone saves you through what He's already done on the cross. Repent, turning from self and sin to Jesus. Tell God and others that your faith is in Jesus.

Offer to talk with any child who is interested in responding to Jesus.

Small Group LEADER

Session Title: Mary Visited Elizabeth
Bible Passage: Luke 1:39-56
Big Picture Question: What was special about Mary's baby? Jesus is God's Son.
Key Passage: Luke 1:76-77
Unit Christ Connection: As prophesied in Isaiah 40:3 and Malachi 3:1, John the Baptist prepared the people for the coming Messiah.

Key passage activity (5 minutes)

- Key Passage Poster
- birthday candles
- masking tape or blank address labels
- marker

Write words or phrases from the key passage on masking tape or blank address labels. Affix the labels to birthday candles and mix them up.

Challenge kids to arrange the key passage correctly. Guide kids to say the passage aloud several times as they work to memorize it.

Say • This key passage is about John, the man God chose to get people ready for Jesus. Through Jesus, God was going to keep His promise to bless all the people in the world.

Bible story review & Bible skills (10 minutes)

- Bibles, 1 per kid
- Small Group Visual Pack

Option: Retell or review the Bible story using the bolded text of the Bible story script.

Review the timeline in the small group visual pack. Help kids recall the previous Bible stories about John the Baptist. Comment that John is called John the Baptist because he grew up and baptized people who repented of their sins.

Help kids find Luke 1:39-56 in their Bibles. Invite volunteers to read verses 39-45 aloud. Then read the following statements and direct kids to choose the true details for each fact.

1. Elizabeth lived on the flat prairie / in the hill country. (*in the hill country, Luke 1:39*)

2. Elizabeth lived alone / with her husband, Zechariah. (*with Zechariah, Luke 1:40*)

3. When Elizabeth's baby heard Mary, he leaped / took a nap. (*leaped, Luke 1:41*)

4. Elizabeth said that Mary and her baby were cursed / blessed. (*blessed, Luke 1:42*)

5. Elizabeth was glad to get a visit from the mother of her Lord / the town doctor. (*the mother of her Lord, Luke 1:43*)

Read Luke 1:46-56 aloud and explain some of the verses from Mary's song.

Say • Mary knew that God is great. God kept the promise He made to Abraham. God had told Abraham that He would bless all the people in the world through Jesus. Jesus would save people from their sins.

• *What was special about Mary's baby? Jesus is God's Son.*

If you choose to review with boys and girls how to become a Christian, explain that kids are welcome to speak with you or another teacher if they have questions.

• **God rules.** God created and is in charge of everything. (Gen. 1:1; Rev. 4:11; Col. 1:16-17)

• **We sinned.** Since Adam and Eve, everyone has chosen to disobey God. (Rom. 3:23; 6:23)

• **God provided.** God sent His Son, Jesus, to rescue us from the punishment we deserve. (John 3:16; Eph. 2:8-9)

• **Jesus gives.** Jesus lived a perfect life, died on the cross for our sins, and rose again so we can be welcomed into God's family. (Rom. 5:8; 2 Cor. 5:21; 1 Pet. 3:18)

• **We respond.** Believe that Jesus alone saves you. Repent. Tell God that your faith is in Jesus. (Rom. 10:9-10,13)

Activity choice (10 minutes)

Option 1: Standing leaps

- masking tape or painter's tape
- adhesive dots
- markers

Use tape to mark a start line on the floor. Mark parallel lines at one-foot intervals. Give each kid an adhesive dot. Provide markers for each kid to write his initials on his dot.

Instruct kids to stand behind the start line. They will take turns leaping past the start line as far as they can. Each kid should use his adhesive dot to mark where he lands. When every kid has had a turn, recognize the kid who leaped the farthest.

If time allows, play again or play a variation of the game by marking intervals on a wall and seeing who can leap the highest. Kids should stand next to the wall and leap as high as they can to position their adhesive dot onto the wall.

Say • You are all great leapers! Even before the babies were born, Elizabeth's baby was happy about Mary's baby. John leaped in Elizabeth's belly when he heard Mary's voice.

• *What was special about Mary's baby? Jesus is God's Son.*

Option 2: Music in a jar

- drinking glasses or glass jars, 5
- water
- spoon
- food color (optional)

Line up five drinking glasses or glass jars and fill them with various amounts of water. If you desire, add different shades of food color to each jar of water. Line up the glasses in order of least full to most full.

Ask kids to guess which glass will produce the highest sound (*least amount of water*) and which will produce the lowest sound (*greatest amount of water*). Demonstrate how to use a spoon to lightly tap on the sides of the glasses to produce different tones.

Allow kids to take turns gently tapping the glasses to produce sounds. Explain that sound is created by vibrations that produce sound waves. Tapping the glass creates vibrations, and the sound waves move through the water. The pitch of the sound—whether it is high or low—depends on how fast the sound waves move. Sound waves move faster in the glasses with less water, so they make higher sounds. Sound waves move slower in the glasses with more water, so they make lower sounds.

Say • Making music is one way we can express how we feel. People often make music when they are happy. Mary praised God with a song because she knew God had given her a very special baby.

• *What was special about Mary's baby? Jesus is God's Son.*

Journal and prayer (5 minutes)

- pencils
- journals
- Bibles
- Journal Page, 1 per kid (enhanced CD)
- "Leap for Joy!" activity page, 1 per kid

Encourage kids to write their own poems or songs on their journal pages. Kids can describe some of the things they know to be true about God. Remind them that Mary praised God with a song because she was so happy.

Say • *What was special about Mary's baby? Jesus is God's Son.*

Invite kids to share prayer requests. Close the group in prayer or allow a couple volunteers to close the group in prayer. As time allows, lead kids to complete the activity page "Leap for Joy!"

Leader BIBLE STUDY

Shortly after Mary left Elizabeth and returned home, the time came for Elizabeth to give birth to her baby. For the duration of Elizabeth's pregnancy, her husband, Zechariah, had been mute. His inability to speak was punishment for his doubting the angel who foretold John's birth. (See Luke 1:20.)

Elizabeth gave birth to a son, and her friends and family rejoiced with her—just as the angel Gabriel had said. (See Luke 1:14.) Everyone had assumed the baby would be named after his father, but Zechariah was clear: HIS NAME IS JOHN.

In Luke 1:66, the people wondered, "What then will this child become?" Zechariah's subsequent prophecy may have answered their question: "And child ... you will go before the Lord to prepare His ways, to give His people knowledge of salvation through the forgiveness of their sins" (Luke 1:76-77).

John would grow up to be an evangelist. He would be spiritually strong. John's ministry would be brief, but through the power of the Holy Spirit, he would lead thousands to repentance. He would humbly prepare the way of the Lord with this aim: "He must increase, but I must decrease" (John 3:30).

John would gain thousands of followers and then joyfully hand them over to Jesus as the groom's friend who rejoices at the groom's voice. John's joy would be complete. (See John 3:29.) Then John would go to prison and ultimately be beheaded by King Herod. But Jesus Himself would say, "Among those born of women no one is greater than John" (Luke 7:28).

As you teach kids the story of John's birth, talk about how John's birth was prophesied by Isaiah. (Isaiah 40:3) Help kids identify who Zechariah was talking about in the first part of his prophecy (*Jesus*, Luke 1:68-75) and the second part of his prophecy (*John*, Luke 1:76-79). John was born to prepare the way for Jesus.

Older Kids BIBLE STUDY OVERVIEW

Session Title: John Was Born
Bible Passage: Luke 1:57-80
Big Picture Question: What role did John the Baptist have in God's plan?
John the Baptist told people to get ready for Jesus, the coming Messiah.
Key Passage: Luke 1:76-77
Unit Christ Connection: As prophesied in Isaiah 40:3 and Malachi 3:1,
John the Baptist prepared the people for the coming Messiah.

U
N
I
T

23

Small Group Opening

Welcome time ....Page 118
Activity page (5 minutes)..Page 118
Session starter (10 minutes) ....Page 118

Large Group Leader

Countdown ....Page 120
Introduce the session (2 minutes) ....Page 120
Timeline map (3 minutes)...Page 120
Big picture question (1 minute) ....Page 121
Tell the Bible story (10 minutes) ....Page 122
The Gospel: God's Plan for Me (optional) ....Page 122
Key passage (4 minutes) ....Page 123
Discussion starter video (5 minutes)...........................Page 123
Sing (3 minutes)...Page 123
Prayer (2 minutes)...Page 124

Small Group Leader

Key passage activity (5 minutes) ....Page 126
Bible story review & Bible skills (10 minutes)...............Page 126
Activity choice (10 minutes)..Page 128
Journal and prayer (5 minutes) ....Page 129

The BIBLE STORY

John Was Born
Luke 1:57-80

The time came for Elizabeth to have her baby. Elizabeth gave birth to a baby boy. Her neighbors and relatives celebrated with Elizabeth because God had given her a good gift: a son.

On the day the baby was to be named, everyone thought Elizabeth and her husband, Zechariah, would name the baby Zechariah. But everyone was wrong.

"We will call him John," Elizabeth said.

Everyone was confused. Usually new parents would name their baby after someone in their family. "None of your relatives has that name," they said.

Then they motioned to Zechariah and asked him what he wanted the baby's name to be. Zechariah couldn't talk; he had been mute since an angel told him Elizabeth was going to have a baby. So **Zechariah asked for a writing tablet. Then he wrote: HIS NAME IS JOHN.**

Everyone was amazed. **All of a sudden, Zechariah could talk again! He began to speak, and he praised God.** Everyone around Zechariah was afraid, and everyone in the hill country in Judah started to talk about what happened. Those who heard about the baby John believed his story, and they said, "What special things will John do in his life?" God was with John.

Then the Holy Spirit filled Zechariah, and God gave Zechariah words to speak. This is what Zechariah said:

> **Praise the Lord, the God of Israel, because He has come and provided the way for His people to be saved.**
>
> **He has raised up a Savior for us from the family of David, just like He said He would do through the prophets long ago.**
>
> He will save us from our enemies.
>
> God was good to our ancestors, and He always kept His promises.
>
> He has allowed us to serve Him without fear.

And you, child—my son—will be a prophet of the Most High.
You will go before the Lord and get the people ready.
You will tell the people about forgiveness and how they can be saved from their sins.

Because God is good and loving, He will send light to those who live in the dark. The light will guide us to the place of peace.

John grew up and became spiritually strong. He lived in the wilderness until the day he appeared to the people in Israel and began to preach and baptize people. He became known as John the Baptist.

Christ Connection: A long time before Jesus was born, prophets said that Jesus would come. The prophets also said another man would come first to say, "Jesus is almost here!" John the Baptist told people to turn away from their sins because Jesus was coming to be King over the whole world.

Small Group OPENING

Session Title: John Was Born
Bible Passage: Luke 1:57-80
Big Picture Question: What role did John the Baptist have in God's plan?
John the Baptist told people to get ready for Jesus, the coming Messiah.
Key Passage: Luke 1:76-77
Unit Christ Connection: As prophesied in Isaiah 40:3 and Malachi 3:1,
John the Baptist prepared the people for the coming Messiah.

Welcome time

• book of names and
their meanings
(optional)

Greet each kid as he or she arrives. Use this time to collect the offering, fill out attendance sheets, and help new kids connect to your group. Ask each kid to share her first and middle names and, if she knows, what they mean.

Activity page (5 minutes)

• "Then and Now"
activity page,
1 per kid
• pencils

Challenge kids to complete the "Then and Now" activity page individually or in pairs. Lead kids to think about the names of their friends, parents, and grandparents. Review the answers as a group.

Say • The popularity of names change over time. The names parents give their children are often quite different than the names your grandparents were given when they were born. In Bible times, parents often named a son after his father.

Session starter (10 minutes)

• chairs

Option 1: Birthday scramble
Arrange chairs in a circle. Use one less chair than the number of kids in your class. Choose one kid to be the caller, and instruct the rest of the kids to sit in the chairs.

The caller will stand in the center of the circle. He will call out two months, such as "April and July." Any kid whose birthday falls in either month should jump up and find an empty chair to sit in. The caller should also try to find a seat. The kid standing without a chair becomes the caller.

On any turn, the caller may say, "Happy birthday, everyone!" Then everyone should jump up to find a new chair. Play several rounds with a new caller each round.

Say • Birthdays are a time to celebrate! People celebrate when a baby is born, and every year friends and family members celebrate another year of life.

• In our Bible story today, friends and family members celebrated the birth of a special baby boy.

Option 2: Buzzing bees

• bottle or jar of honey

Play a hot-and-cold game. Select a volunteer to be the "bear." The rest of the kids will be the "bees." Show the honey and tell kids that you will hide it in the room. The bear will try to find the honey. If the bear gets close to the hidden honey, the bees should buzz loudly. If the bear moves away from the honey, the bees should buzz quietly.

Instruct the bear to step into the hallway with an adult helper, and then hide the honey in the room. Call the bear back inside and encourage the bees to guide the bear by buzzing loudly or quietly. Play multiple rounds if time allows.

Say • In today's Bible story, we will hear about a boy God chose for a special job. He grew up and started preaching in the wilderness. While he was in the wilderness, he ate locusts and wild honey.

Transition to large group

Large Group LEADER

Session Title: John Was Born
Bible Passage: Luke 1:57-80
Big Picture Question: What role did John the Baptist have in God's plan?
John the Baptist told people to get ready for Jesus, the coming Messiah.
Key Passage: Luke 1:76-77
Unit Christ Connection: As prophesied in Isaiah 40:3 and Malachi 3:1,
John the Baptist prepared the people for the coming Messiah.

Countdown

• countdown video

Show the countdown video as your kids arrive, and set it to end as large group time begins.

Introduce the session (2 minutes)

• gift-wrapped box

[Large Group Leader enters carrying a box covered in gift wrap.]

Leader • Hello there! Welcome! I'm [*your name*], party planner extraordinaire! Today is the day! We have decorations, tasty food, and party games. It is time to celebrate a birthday!

Does anyone here have a birthday today? Raise your hand if you have a birthday this month. What about next month? Or last month? Well, happy birthday to all of you! I am very glad you were born. Unfortunately, this party isn't for you. Do you know whose birthday we are celebrating today? The answer is in today's Bible story.

Timeline map (3 minutes)

• Timeline Map

Remember to point to each story on the timeline as you review.

Leader • Let's see here ... "Genealogy of Jesus," "John's

Birth Was Predicted," and "Mary Visited Elizabeth." So far we have learned that God had been working out His plan to send Jesus since the beginning. God had made a promise to Abraham that He would bless the whole world through one of Abraham's descendants. That descendant is Jesus! Jesus was part of Abraham's family. Jesus' true Father is God, but the Bible tells us about many people who were part of Jesus' earthly family. Do you remember, *How is Jesus different from any other man? Jesus is fully God and fully man.*

John was also part of God's plan. *Who announced John's birth? The angel Gabriel told Zechariah that he would have a son.* Gabriel also told Mary that she would have a baby.

Mary was Jesus' mom, and Elizabeth was John's mom. Mary and Elizabeth were relatives. Every baby is special, but there was something extra special about Mary's baby. *What was special about Mary's baby? Jesus is God's Son.* We celebrate Jesus' birthday at Christmas, so today's party must be for John! God had a special purpose for John's life.

Big picture question (1 minute)

• Bibles, 1 per kid

Leader • God planned for John to have an important job. We call John "John the Baptist" because he baptized people who repented of their sin. That leads me to our big picture question. Our big picture question is, *What role did John the Baptist have in God's plan?* That is a very good question. Listen carefully to the Bible story and see if you can figure out the answer.

Guide kids to find Luke 1 in their Bibles. Remind them that the Book of Luke is one of the Gospels.

Leader • Can you name all four Gospels? (*Matthew, Mark,*

Luke, John) The Gospels tell us about Jesus' life, death, and resurrection.

Tell the Bible story (10 minutes)

- "John Was Born" video
- Bibles
- Bible Story Picture Slide or Poster
- Big Picture Question Slide or Poster

Open your Bible to Luke 1:57-80 and tell the Bible story in your own words, or show the Bible story video "John Was Born."

Leader • Elizabeth gave birth to a son, just like the angel Gabriel had said would happen. And everyone was happy! Zechariah and Elizabeth needed to give the baby a name. Their friends and family thought they would name him after Zechariah. Zechariah Jr.? No. Elizabeth said, "We will call him John." Zechariah wrote on a tablet and showed that he too wanted to name the baby John.

Zechariah hadn't been able to speak ever since Gabriel announced the baby, but now he could talk again! Zechariah praised God. The Holy Spirit gave Zechariah words to speak. Zechariah said that God had great plans for John. John grew up and went into the wilderness when it was time for him to start working for God.

What is our big picture question? *What role did John the Baptist have in God's plan? John the Baptist told people to get ready for Jesus, the coming Messiah.* Say the big picture question and answer with me. *What role did John the Baptist have in God's plan? John the Baptist told people to get ready for Jesus, the coming Messiah.*

The Gospel: God's Plan for Me (optional)

Using Scripture and the guide provided, explain to boys and girls how to become a Christian. Tell kids how they can respond, and provide counselors to speak with each kid individually. Guide counselors to use open-ended questions to allow kids to determine the direction of the conversation.

Encourage boys and girls to ask their parents, small group leaders, or other adults any questions they may have about becoming a Christian.

Key passage (4 minutes)

• Key Passage Slide or Poster
• "You Will Be Called" song

Leader • Our key passage is the place we find the answer to our big picture question. Zechariah said that John would go before the Lord and get people ready for Jesus. Can anyone say the key passage from memory?

Give volunteers the opportunity to recite the key passage. Then lead everyone to say it together. Sing "You Will Be Called."

Discussion starter video (5 minutes)

• "Unit 23 Session 4" discussion starter video

Leader • So, according to our big picture question and answer, *What role did John the Baptist have in God's plan? John the Baptist told people to get ready for Jesus, the coming Messiah.* God had a special plan for John's life. Did you know that God has a plan for your life too? Let's watch this video.

Show the "Unit 23 Session 4" video. Then prompt kids to share what they want to be when they grow up.

Leader • We often make our own plans, but God already knows how He wants to use us to tell others about Jesus. His plans are perfect! We can pray and ask God to guide our futures so we can be obedient to His wonderful plans.

Sing (3 minutes)

• "Ready or Not" song

Leader • God's people had been looking forward to Jesus for a long time. The Old Testament prophets had told about a Messiah who would come to save people from their sin. The people waited hundreds of years for God to send the Messiah. When John was born, God already had a special plan for his life. John would tell people, "The Messiah is almost here!" That must have been great news for the people who had been waiting so long. Maybe they praised God. We can praise God today with our theme song. Let's sing it together.

Lead boys and girls to sing "Ready or Not."

Prayer (2 minutes)

- Allergy Alert (enhanced CD)
- small bags of snacks or party favors

Post an allergy alert prior to the start of large group time. Provide small bags of snacks or party favors for kids to take with them.

Leader • Thank you, everyone, for coming to the party! I had a lot of fun celebrating John's birthday with you. I'm going to pray, and then you can follow your small group leader to learn more about John; you might even play a party game!

Close in prayer. Thank God for sending John to get people ready for Jesus and to teach them how to be forgiven for their sins. Thank Him for Jesus, who died on the cross to pay for our sins. Ask God to help kids tell others the good news about Jesus so others can be forgiven too.

Dismiss to small groups

The Gospel: God's Plan for Me

Ask kids if they have ever heard the word *gospel*. Clarify that the word *gospel* means "good news." It is the message about Christ, the kingdom of God, and salvation. Use the following guide to share the gospel with kids.

God rules. Explain to kids that the Bible tells us God created everything, and He is in charge of everything. Invite a volunteer to read Genesis 1:1 from the Bible. Read Revelation 4:11 or Colossians 1:16-17 aloud and explain what these verses mean.

We sinned. Tell kids that since the time of Adam and Eve, everyone has chosen to disobey God. (Romans 3:23) The Bible calls this sin. Because God is holy, God cannot be around sin. Sin separates us from God and deserves God's punishment of death. (Romans 6:23)

God provided. Choose a child to read John 3:16 aloud. Say that God sent His Son, Jesus, the perfect solution to our sin problem, to rescue us from the punishment we deserve. It's something we, as sinners, could never earn on our own. Jesus alone saves us. Read and explain Ephesians 2:8-9.

Jesus gives. Share with kids that Jesus lived a perfect life, died on the cross for our sins, and rose again. Because Jesus gave up His life for us, we can be welcomed into God's family for eternity. This is the best gift ever! Read Romans 5:8; 2 Corinthians 5:21; or 1 Peter 3:18.

We respond. Tell kids that they can respond to Jesus. Read Romans 10:9-10,13. Review these aspects of our response: Believe in your heart that Jesus alone saves you through what He's already done on the cross. Repent, turning from self and sin to Jesus. Tell God and others that your faith is in Jesus.

Offer to talk with any child who is interested in responding to Jesus.

Small Group LEADER

Session Title: John Was Born
Bible Passage: Luke 1:57-80
Big Picture Question: What role did John the Baptist have in God's plan?
John the Baptist told people to get ready for Jesus, the coming Messiah.
Key Passage: Luke 1:76-77
Unit Christ Connection: As prophesied in Isaiah 40:3 and Malachi 3:1,
John the Baptist prepared the people for the coming Messiah.

Key passage activity (5 minutes)

- Key Passage Poster
- slips of paper
- tape
- marker

Before the small group time, write phrases of the key passage on several slips of paper and tape them to various objects around the room.

Explain to kids that the key passage is hidden on objects throughout the room. Invite kids to search for the passage and collect the labeled items. Then kids should work together to arrange the passage in the correct order. When kids finish, choose a volunteer to lead the class in saying the key passage aloud three times.

Say • Very good! The Holy Spirit spoke through Zechariah and revealed God's big plan for John's life.

Bible story review & Bible skills (10 minutes)

- Bibles, 1 per kid
- Small Group Visual Pack

Guide kids to find Luke 1:57-80 in their Bibles. Ask kids to identify the testament and Bible division in which the passage is located. (*New Testament, Gospels*) Lead kids to read Luke 1:57-66 aloud, taking turns reading one verse at a time.

Read the following statements. If kids think the statement is true, they should shout, "Happy birthday!" If the statement is false, kids should say, "No way!"

1. Elizabeth gave birth to a son. (*true, Luke 1:57*)
2. Elizabeth said that the baby's name was John. (*true, Luke 1:60*)
3. Zechariah wrote: His name is Zechariah Jr. (*false, Luke 1:63*)
4. Zechariah was able to speak again (*true, Luke 1:64*)
5. God was with John. (*true, Luke 1:66*)

Read Luke 1:67-80 aloud, or use the bolded portions of the Bible story script to provide a summary of Zechariah's prophecy.

Say • God gave Zechariah words to speak, and the words were about God's plan for John.

• ***What role did John the Baptist have in God's plan? John the Baptist told people to get ready for Jesus, the coming Messiah.***

If you choose to review with boys and girls how to become a Christian, explain that kids are welcome to speak with you or another teacher if they have questions.

• **God rules.** God created and is in charge of everything. (Gen. 1:1; Rev. 4:11; Col. 1:16-17)

• **We sinned.** Since Adam and Eve, everyone has chosen to disobey God. (Rom. 3:23; 6:23)

• **God provided.** God sent His Son, Jesus, to rescue us from the punishment we deserve. (John 3:16; Eph. 2:8-9)

• **Jesus gives.** Jesus lived a perfect life, died on the cross for our sins, and rose again so we can be welcomed into God's family. (Rom. 5:8; 2 Cor. 5:21; 1 Pet. 3:18)

• **We respond.** Believe that Jesus alone saves you. Repent. Tell God that your faith is in Jesus. (Rom. 10:9-10,13)

• chalkboard or black
construction paper
• chalk

Activity choice (10 minutes)

Option 1: Writing tablet relay

Form two teams and instruct kids to line up single file behind the start line. Position a chalkboard or sheet of black construction paper and a stick of chalk across the room from each team.

Explain the rules. Teams will race to write the sentence *HIS NAME IS JOHN* on the chalkboard. Kids may only write one letter at a time.

When you say go, the first kid for each team will race to the chalkboard, pick up the chalk, and write the letter *H*. He should carry the chalk back to the start line and pass it to the next player. The second player will run to the chalkboard and add the letter *I*. The first team to accurately complete the sentence should sit down behind the start line.

Say • John was born with a very important job. ***What role did John the Baptist have in God's plan? John the Baptist told people to get ready for Jesus, the coming Messiah.***

Option 2: Landscape drawings

• paper
• markers, crayons, or
colored pencils

Give each kid a piece of paper. Provide markers, crayons, or colored pencils. Give kids two options for drawing: they may draw a highway in a desert, or they may draw a forest. Allow several minutes for kids to draw. Encourage them to add as many details as they desire.

Invite volunteers to share their drawings with the class. Point out whether the highway drawings are curved highways or straight highways.

Say • Some of the prophets in the Old Testament talked about John before he was born. One of those prophets was the prophet Isaiah. [*Read Isaiah 40:3 aloud from your Bible.*]

> *What role did John the Baptist have in God's plan?
> John the Baptist told people to get ready for Jesus,
> the coming Messiah.*

Journal and prayer (5 minutes)

- pencils
- journals
- Bibles
- Journal Page, 1 per kid (enhanced CD)
- "Hidden Dot Message" activity page, 1 per kid

Distribute journal pages to the kids. Guide each kid to write about or draw a picture of a job she would like to have someday.

Say • *What role did John the Baptist have in God's plan? John the Baptist told people to get ready for Jesus, the coming Messiah.* God can use people in all sorts of different jobs as part of His plan.

Invite kids to share prayer requests. Close the group in prayer or allow a couple of volunteers to close the group in prayer.

Pray: "God, You had a plan for John's life, and we know that you have a plan for us, too. Your plans are perfect. Help us trust in You and tell others the good news about Jesus so everyone will be ready when Jesus comes again. We love you. Amen."

If time allows, lead kids to complete the activity page "Hidden Dot Message."

Leader BIBLE STUDY

God is in control of all things. Was it by chance that Caesar Augustus called for a census? Did it just so happen that Mary and Joseph were traveling to Bethlehem—the very place the Messiah was prophesied to be born? (Mic. 5:2) God used a pagan emperor to bring about His plan.

God's plan was for Jesus to be born in a manger. A king born in a manger! It was so unlikely. But Jesus was no ordinary baby; He was God's Son, sent in the most humble of circumstances, "not to be served, but to serve, and to give His life—a ransom for many" (Matt. 20:28).

Imagine the shepherds' surprise when an angel of the Lord suddenly appeared. They were terrified! But the angel said to them, "Don't be afraid, for look, I proclaim to you good news of great joy that will be for all the people: Today a Savior, who is Messiah the Lord, was born for you in the city of David" (Luke 2:10-11).

What a relief! This angel had good news. First, he proclaimed a Savior. The people of Israel were well aware of their need for a Savior. They made sacrifices daily to atone for their sin. Finally, a Savior had come who would be the perfect sacrifice for sin, once and for all. Jesus is also Messiah the Lord.

The word *Messiah* means "anointed one," especially a king. The Deliverer and Redeemer would be King over His people. And this was all happening in Bethlehem, the city of David—just as the prophet Micah said.

This is the best news ever! An army of angels appeared, praising God and saying: "Glory to God in the highest heaven, and peace on earth to people He favors" (Luke 2:14). The purpose of Jesus' birth was twofold: to bring glory to God and to make peace between God and those who trusted in Jesus' death and resurrection to provide salvation.

Older Kids BIBLE STUDY OVERVIEW

Session Title: Jesus Was Born

Bible Passage: Luke 2:1-20

Big Picture Question: Why was Jesus born? Jesus was born to be God's promised Savior.

Key Passage: John 1:14

Unit Christ Connection: Old Testament prophecies looked forward to the birth of Christ. Jesus' roles as Son of God and Messiah are established.

Small Group Opening

Welcome time ....Page 134

Activity page (5 minutes)...Page 134

Session starter (10 minutes)...Page 134

Large Group Leader

Countdown...Page 136

Introduce the session (3 minutes) ....Page 136

Timeline map (1 minute)...Page 137

Big picture question (1 minute) ....Page 137

Tell the Bible story (10 minutes) ....Page 137

The Gospel: God's Plan for Me (optional) ....Page 139

Key passage (5 minutes) ....Page 139

Discussion starter video (5 minutes)...............................Page 139

Sing (3 minutes)...Page 140

Prayer (2 minutes)...Page 140

Small Group Leader

Key passage activity (5 minutes) ....Page 142

Bible story review & Bible skills (10 minutes)................Page 143

Activity choice (10 minutes)...Page 144

Journal and prayer (5 minutes) ....Page 145

The BIBLE STORY

Jesus Was Born
Luke 2:1-20

During the time Mary was pregnant with Baby Jesus, the Roman emperor, Caesar Augustus, **announced that everyone needed to be registered for a census.** Every person traveled to the town where his family was from. **Since Joseph was a descendant of King David, he and Mary left Nazareth and traveled to Bethlehem, the city of David.**

While they were there, the time came for Mary to have her baby. Mary and Joseph looked for a safe place for Mary to have her baby, but **every place was full because of all the people who were in town to be counted. So Mary and Joseph found a place where animals were kept, and that is where Mary had her baby, Jesus.** She wrapped Him snugly in cloth, and she laid Him in a feeding trough, where the animals ate their food.

In the same region, some shepherds were staying out in the fields and watching their sheep to protect them from thieves and predators. **All of a sudden, an angel of the Lord stood before them. A bright light shone around the shepherds, and they were terrified!**

But the angel said to them, "Don't be afraid! I have very good news for you: Today a Savior, who is Messiah the Lord, was born for you in the city of David." Then the angel said, "You will find a baby wrapped snugly in cloth and lying in a feeding trough." A king in a feeding trough? That was no place for a king!

All of a sudden, a whole army of angels appeared, praising God and saying, "Glory to God in the highest heaven, and peace on earth to people He favors!"

So the shepherds went straight to Bethlehem to find Baby Jesus. They found Mary and Joseph, and the baby who was lying in the feeding trough. The shepherds went and told others about the baby Jesus. Everyone who heard about Jesus was surprised and amazed. Mary thought about everything that was happening and tried to understand it. The shepherds returned to their fields, praising God because everything had happened just as the angel had said.

Christ Connection: The birth of Jesus was good news! Jesus was not an ordinary baby. He is God's Son, sent to earth from heaven. Jesus came into the world to save people from their sins and to be their King.

Small Group OPENING

Session Title: Jesus Was Born
Bible Passage: Luke 2:1-20
Big Picture Question: Why was Jesus born? Jesus was born to be God's promised Savior.
Key Passage: John 1:14
Unit Christ Connection: Old Testament prophecies looked forward to the birth of Christ. Jesus' roles as Son of God and Messiah are established.

Welcome time

Greet each kid as he or she arrives. Use this time to collect the offering, fill out attendance sheets, and help new kids connect to your group. Ask kids to share their favorite birthday memories.

Activity page (5 minutes)

• "Poll Party" activity page, 1 per kid
• pencils

Guide each kid to write his or her name at the top of the "Poll Party" activity page. Announce that kids should move around and survey their classmates to find out their birthdays. Each kid may sign his name in the box labeled with his birthday month. Challenge kids to collect as many signatures as they can in two minutes.

Say • Every year, you celebrate your birthday, the day you were born. Whose birthday do we celebrate on Christmas? That's right—Jesus'!

Session starter (10 minutes)

Option 1: Sheep and wolves

Form groups of four kids. In each group, assign one wolf, one sheep, and two shepherds. Instruct the shepherds and sheep to join hands, forming a triangle. The wolf must stand outside the group. The goal of the game is for the wolf to tag the sheep. The shepherds can spin around—without letting go of their hands—to keep the sheep away from the wolf. If the wolf is able to tag the sheep, let the players switch roles and play again.

Say • Wolves are predators; they eat sheep for lunch! In the Bible story today, some shepherds were in their fields, protecting their sheep from predators. But they heard news that a Savior was born! They left their sheep and hurried to find Him.

Option 2: Census count

• "Group Census Sheet," 1 per group (enhanced CD)
• pencils

Form groups of two to ten kids. Groups do not need to have equal numbers of kids. Provide one kid in each group with a copy of the group census sheet. She should interview the others in her group to record the required census data. Census takers should also include data about themselves.

Give kids a few minutes to collect census data and list the totals on the census sheet. Prompt each group to examine which group member is the youngest. Who is the oldest? How many of the group members were born in another state? When kids finish, collect the census sheets. Announce some of the data totals. How many boys are in the class? How many girls?

Say • Great work, everyone. Census data is helpful in learning about who is living in certain areas.
• In our Bible story today, the Roman emperor— Caesar Augustus—conducted a census so he would have a list of people he could collect taxes from. All the people had to travel to their hometowns to be counted.

Transition to large group

Large Group LEADER

Session Title: Jesus Was Born
Bible Passage: Luke 2:1-20
Big Picture Question: Why was Jesus born? Jesus was born to be God's promised Savior.
Key Passage: John 1:14
Unit Christ Connection: Old Testament prophecies looked forward to the birth of Christ. Jesus' roles as Son of God and Messiah are established.

• room decorations

Tip: Select decorations that fit your ministry and budget.

Suggested Theme Decorating Ideas: Simulate a photography studio by hanging white paper or a bedsheet as a backdrop. Set a stool in front of the backdrop, and position a few spotlights or lamps around the teaching area. Consider arranging various props nearby, such as picture frames, portraits, photo albums, and a tripod.

Countdown

• countdown video

Show the countdown video as your kids arrive, and set it to end as large group time begins.

Introduce the session (3 minutes)

• camera or camera phone

[Large Group Leader carrying a camera or camera phone.]

Leader • Hello, everyone! I'm so glad you're here. My name is [*your name*], and this is my camera. I haven't been using it very long, but I'd be happy to teach you some of the tips I've learned about photography. Raise your hand if you have ever taken a photograph.

Wow! Most of you! Well, you're already ahead of the game. Fortunately a lot of cameras these days are digital. When I was growing up, we took photos using film. You had to get your film developed before you could even see your photos. These days, your photos are ready instantly.

Older Kids Bible Study Leader Guide
Unit 24 • Session 1

Do you know when the first photo was made? The first photos were made in France in the early 1800s—more than 175 years ago! Before that, if you wanted a picture of someone, you had to draw or paint a picture. I sure am thankful for today's technology!

So we're going to learn a little bit about photography the next few times we meet, and hopefully by the end, you'll be a few steps closer to being true photographers!

Now that you've heard about when cameras began, let's get ready for today's Bible story. It's a story about how Jesus' life on earth began.

Timeline map (1 minute)

• Timeline Map

Point to today's Bible story, "Jesus Was Born," on the timeline map.

Leader • Here we are on our timeline map. So many of the events in the Old Testament were leading up to this point! God had promised to send someone to help His people. The people were slaves to sin; no matter how hard they tried, they couldn't keep from sinning. That's why God sent Jesus.

Big picture question (1 minute)

Leader • Our big picture question is, *Why was Jesus born?* If you think you know the answer, don't say it just yet. Pay close attention to the Bible story to see if you're correct.

• "Jesus Was Born" video
• Bibles, 1 per kid
• Bible Story Picture Slide or Poster
• Big Picture Question Slide or Poster

Tell the Bible story (10 minutes)

Open your Bible to Luke 2 and tell the Bible story in your own words, or show the Bible story video "Jesus Was Born." Invite volunteers to retell the story in their own words. Ask review questions to test kids' listening skills.

Tip: A Bible story
script is provided
at the beginning of
every session. You
may use it to guide
you as you prepare
to teach the Bible
story in your own
words. For a shorter
version of the Bible
story, read only the
bolded text.

Leader • What was the name of the Roman emperor?
(*Caesar Augustus, Luke 2:1*)

• What town did Mary and Joseph travel to?
(*Bethlehem, Luke 2:4*)

• Why did Mary have her baby in a manger? (*There
was no room in the inn, Luke 2:7*)

• What were the shepherds doing in the fields?
(*watching over their sheep, Luke 2:8*)

• Who appeared the the shepherds? (*an angel of the
Lord, Luke 2:9*)

• What news did the angel give the shepherds? (*good
news, a Savior was born in Bethlehem; Luke 2:10-11*)

• Where did the angel say the shepherds would find the
baby? (*lying in a feeding trough, Luke 2:12*)

• What did the shepherds do after seeing Jesus? (*told
others, glorified and praised God; Luke 2:17,20*)

• **Why was Jesus born? Jesus was born to be God's
promised Savior.**

Review the big picture question and answer with kids.

Leader • *Why was Jesus born? Jesus was born to be
God's promised Savior.*

That's right. Jesus is the promised Savior the Old
Testament prophets had spoken about. He is God's plan to
save people from their sin.

Everyone sins, or disobeys God. We deserve to be
punished for our sin, and the punishment for sin is death
and eternal separation from God. But God loves us so
much that He sent Jesus to save us from sin. Jesus took
our punishment on the cross by dying the death we
deserve, and then God raised Him from the dead. When
we trust Jesus as Lord and Savior, God forgives our sin so
we can be with Him forever.

The Gospel: God's Plan for Me (optional)

Using Scripture and the guide provided, explain to boys and girls how to become a Christian. Tell kids how they can respond, and provide counselors to speak with each kid individually. Guide counselors to use open-ended questions to allow kids to determine the direction of the conversation.

Encourage boys and girls to ask their parents, small group leaders, or other adults any questions they may have about becoming a Christian.

Key passage (5 minutes)

- Key Passage Slide or Poster
- "Grace and Truth" song

Leader • Our key passage is from the Book of John. John is the fourth book in the New Testament. Do you know which Bible division John is part of? That's right, the Gospels. Can you name all four Gospels? (*Matthew, Mark, Luke, John*)

These verses tell us about Jesus. John's Gospel is all about Jesus' life on earth. Another name for Jesus is *the Word*. Jesus' words and life would tell people what God is like. Let's read the passage together.

Sing together "Grace and Truth."

Discussion starter video (5 minutes)

- "Unit 24 Session 1" discussion starter video

Leader • What are some things you like to do to celebrate your birthday? Maybe you invite friends over, play games, and eat tasty food. Check out this video.

Show the "Unit 24 Session 1" video.

Leader • Yikes! Kids *eat* cupcakes at birthday parties! What are your favorite birthday foods?

Whose birthday do we celebrate at Christmas? Yes! We celebrate Jesus' birth because His birth brought hope to the world. ***Why was Jesus born? Jesus was born to be God's promised Savior.***

Sing (3 minutes)

• "In Jesus' Name" song

Leader • The birth of Jesus is certainly a reason to celebrate! One way we can celebrate is by singing songs to praise God. Stand with me and let's sing our theme song.

Lead boys and girls to sing "In Jesus' Name."

Prayer (2 minutes)

Leader • I am really glad you came today. We learned that photography got its start long ago. The beginning of photography changed everything about how we record our memories. Jesus' life on earth began Bethlehem—in a manger—and His birth changed everything because of why He was born. *Why was Jesus born? Jesus was born to be God's promised Savior.*

Close in prayer. Pray: "Lord, thank You for keeping Your promises and for sending Jesus to be our Savior. Help us trust in Him, and help us tell others about Jesus so their sins can be forgiven too. Amen."

Dismiss to small groups

The Gospel: God's Plan for Me

Ask kids if they have ever heard the word *gospel*. Clarify that the word *gospel* means "good news." It is the message about Christ, the kingdom of God, and salvation. Use the following guide to share the gospel with kids.

God rules. Explain to kids that the Bible tells us God created everything, and He is in charge of everything. Invite a volunteer to read Genesis 1:1 from the Bible. Read Revelation 4:11 or Colossians 1:16-17 aloud and explain what these verses mean.

We sinned. Tell kids that since the time of Adam and Eve, everyone has chosen to disobey God. (Romans 3:23) The Bible calls this sin. Because God is holy, God cannot be around sin. Sin separates us from God and deserves God's punishment of death. (Romans 6:23)

God provided. Choose a child to read John 3:16 aloud. Say that God sent His Son, Jesus, the perfect solution to our sin problem, to rescue us from the punishment we deserve. It's something we, as sinners, could never earn on our own. Jesus alone saves us. Read and explain Ephesians 2:8-9.

Jesus gives. Share with kids that Jesus lived a perfect life, died on the cross for our sins, and rose again. Because Jesus gave up His life for us, we can be welcomed into God's family for eternity. This is the best gift ever! Read Romans 5:8; 2 Corinthians 5:21; or 1 Peter 3:18.

We respond. Tell kids that they can respond to Jesus. Read Romans 10:9-10,13. Review these aspects of our response: Believe in your heart that Jesus alone saves you through what He's already done on the cross. Repent, turning from self and sin to Jesus. Tell God and others that your faith is in Jesus.

Offer to talk with any child who is interested in responding to Jesus.

Small Group LEADER

Session Title: Jesus Was Born
Bible Passage: Luke 2:1-20
Big Picture Question: Why was Jesus born? Jesus was born to be God's promised Savior.
Key Passage: John 1:14
Unit Christ Connection: Old Testament prophecies looked forward to the birth of Christ. Jesus' roles as Son of God and Messiah are established.

Key passage activity (5 minutes)

• Key Passage Poster

Display the key passage or guide kids to look at it in their Bibles. Encourage them to learn the following motions for key words to act out as they recite the passage:

1. *Word*: palms together, then open like a book
2. *flesh*: hold hands in front of you and turn palms up and down to show your skin
3. *among*: hold palms up at your side and turn hips right and left
4. *seen/observed*: curl fingers around eyes like binoculars
5. *One and Only*: hold up one finger
6. *Father*: spread five fingers and touch thumb to forehead
7. *truth*: use hands to form a *T* shape

Demonstrate each action and help kids practice them several times. Then lead them to say the key passage while performing the actions for the key words.

Say • Wow! Great job, everyone. This key passage says that the Word [*perform action*]—which is Jesus—became flesh [*perform action*], or a man, and came to live among [*perform action*] God's people.

Bible story review & Bible skills (10 minutes)

- Bibles, 1 per kid
- chalkboards and chalk, dry erase boards and markers, or paper and markers
- Small Group Visual Pack

Option: Retell or review the Bible story using the bolded text of the Bible story script.

Form two teams. For each team, provide chalk and a chalkboard, dry erase markers and a whiteboard, or markers and a large piece of paper attached to a focal wall.

Guide each team to pick a runner. Teams will pick a new runner each round. Explain that you will read a statement about today's Bible story. Teams should look at Luke 2 in their Bibles to find the verse that supports the statement. A team should tell its runner the verse number, and then the runner will race to the chalkboard and write the reference. Encourage kids to write the entire reference, including Bible book, chapter number, and verse number. The first runner to write the correct answer earns his team one point.

Help kids find Luke 2 in their Bibles before you begin.

Say • The time came for Mary to have her baby. (*Luke 2:6*)
- The angels said, "Glory to God in the highest!" (*Luke 2:14*)
- The shepherds found Mary, Joseph, and the baby. (*Luke 2:16*)
- Joseph was part of David's family. (*Luke 2:4*)
- Mary wrapped Jesus snuggly in cloth. (*Luke 2:7*)
- Caesar Augustus ordered everyone to be registered (*Luke 2:1*)
- The angel told the shepherds to not be afraid. (*Luke 2:10*)

Review the timeline map in the small group visual pack to remind kids of the big picture of God's plan to send Jesus.

Say • *Why was Jesus born? Jesus was born to be God's promised Savior.*

If you choose to review with boys and girls how to become a Christian, explain that kids are welcome to speak with you or another teacher if they have questions.

- **God rules.** God created and is in charge of

everything. (Gen. 1:1; Rev. 4:11; Col. 1:16-17)

- **We sinned.** Since Adam and Eve, everyone has chosen to disobey God. (Rom. 3:23; 6:23)
- **God provided.** God sent His Son, Jesus, to rescue us from the punishment we deserve. (John 3:16; Eph. 2:8-9)
- **Jesus gives.** Jesus lived a perfect life, died on the cross for our sins, and rose again so we can be welcomed into God's family. (Rom. 5:8; 2 Cor. 5:21; 1 Pet. 3:18)
- **We respond.** Believe that Jesus alone saves you. Repent. Tell God that your faith is in Jesus. (Rom. 10:9-10,13)

Activity choice (10 minutes)

- large piece of paper
- crayons or markers

Option 1: "Fit for a king" mural

Attach a large piece of paper to the wall or lay it out on a long table. Provide crayons or markers. Invite kids to work together to design a house for a king. Prompt them to consider how many rooms the house will have and what type of furniture will be in the house. Guide kids to include the king's room. What would it look like? Where would the king sleep?

Say • Kings deserve the best because they often have a lot of responsibilities as they rule over a country or group of people. Kings have power, and they usually live in nice palaces.

- Jesus is a king unlike any other king. When He was born, He didn't live in a palace. He was born in a place where animals are kept. Jesus came for a special purpose.
- *Why was Jesus born? Jesus was born to be God's promised Savior.*

Option 2: Breaking news drama

- paper
- pencils
- Bible times clothing and other props (optional)

Form groups of four or more kids. Instruct kids to review Luke 2:8-20 and use the Bible passage as a guide. Invite kids to imagine the shepherds who visited Jesus were interviewed by the local news agency. Each group of kids should choose one reporter to interview the rest of the group (the shepherds) and ask them questions about their experience looking for the baby Jesus.

As kids prepare, encourage them to make a list of interview questions and practice their skit once or twice before performing it for the rest of the class. If kids need help thinking of interview questions, provide some suggestions: Where were you when the angel appeared? Were you scared? What were the angels saying? Did you find Jesus? What did you do next?

Say • You are very good journalists! Asking questions is one way to learn new information. Let's review our big picture question one more time. ***Why was Jesus born? Jesus was born to be God's promised Savior.***

Journal and prayer (5 minutes)

- pencils
- journals
- Bibles
- Journal Page, 1 per kid (enhanced CD)
- "Comic Strip Story" activity page, 1 per kid

Lead each kid to write or draw a picture on her journal page about a time she received good news. Ask kids to express how the good news made them feel. What did they do when they heard the news?

Say • ***Why was Jesus born? Jesus was born to be God's promised Savior.*** That is some very good news! Invite kids to share prayer requests. Close the group in prayer or allow a couple of volunteers to close the group in prayer. Thank God for sending Jesus as the promised Savior.

As time allows, lead kids to complete the activity page "Comic Strip Story."

Leader BIBLE STUDY

The Lord spoke to Moses: "Consecrate every firstborn male to Me, the firstborn from every womb among the Israelites, both man and domestic animal; it is Mine" (Ex. 13:2).

Consecrate means "to dedicate to a sacred purpose." God's people were to set apart their firstborn as belonging to the Lord. The firstborn of sacrificial animals were sacrificed to God, and the firstborn of humans and donkeys were redeemed—a lamb was sacrificed instead. God's law for the consecration of the firstborn had a purpose: to remind the people that the Lord brought them out of Egypt by the strength of His hand. (See Ex. 13:14-16.)

After a woman gave birth, she was "unclean," and she would observe a period of purification—a reminder that we are all born in sin. Then she would bring to the priest a young lamb for a burnt offering and a young pigeon or turtledove for a sin offering. (See Lev. 12:1-6.) If a woman could not afford a sheep for the sacrifice, the law allowed her to take two pigeons or two turtledoves instead. (Lev. 12:8)

This is what Mary did. When Mary's days of purification were complete, Mary and Joseph took Jesus to Jerusalem, where they presented Him to the Lord and offered a sacrifice. Though Jesus was not born in sin, He identified with sinners even as a baby. This initial act introduced Jesus' perfect life of obedience to the law.

While Mary and Joseph were at the temple, God graciously revealed to a man named Simeon and a woman named Anna that Jesus was the One—the promised Messiah they had been waiting for. Imagine their joy. At last!

Today, we can have faith in Jesus and His finished work on the cross for our salvation. When God opens our eyes to the good news of the gospel, we can live and die in peace, for our eyes have seen His salvation.

Older Kids BIBLE STUDY OVERVIEW

Session Title: Jesus Was Dedicated

Bible Passage: Luke 2:21-40

Big Picture Question: Why were Simeon and Anna waiting? Simeon and Anna were waiting for God to keep His promise to send Jesus to save them from their sins.

Key Passage: John 1:14

Unit Christ Connection: Old Testament prophecies looked forward to the birth of Christ. Jesus' roles as Son of God and Messiah are established.

Small Group Opening

Welcome time ....Page 150

Activity page (5 minutes)..Page 150

Session starter (10 minutes) ....Page 150

Large Group Leader

Countdown..Page 152

Introduce the session (3 minutes) ....Page 152

Timeline map (1 minute)...Page 153

Big picture question (1 minute) ....Page 153

Tell the Bible story (10 minutes) ....Page 153

The Gospel: God's Plan for Me (optional) ....Page 154

Key passage (5 minutes) ....Page 155

Discussion starter video (4 minutes)...............................Page 155

Sing (4 minutes)..Page 156

Prayer (2 minutes)...Page 156

Small Group Leader

Key passage activity (5 minutes) ....Page 158

Bible story review & Bible skills (10 minutes)................Page 158

Activity choice (10 minutes)...Page 160

Journal and prayer (5 minutes) ....Page 161

The BIBLE STORY

Jesus Was Dedicated
Luke 2:21-40

Mary and Joseph's baby—God's Son—was a few days old when Mary and Joseph named Him Jesus, just like the angel had told them to do before the baby was even born. One day, Mary and Joseph **took Jesus to the temple in Jerusalem.**

Mary and Joseph wanted to obey God and His law. Part of the law that God gave Moses said, "When a woman's first son is born, his parents must dedicate him to the Lord." The law also said that the child's parents should sacrifice two turtledoves or two young pigeons for the child. **At the temple, Mary and Joseph presented Jesus to the Lord and offered two birds as a sacrifice.**

Another man was at the temple. His name was Simeon, and he lived in Jerusalem. Simeon loved God, and He trusted in God's promise to send a Messiah to save people from sin. **God's Spirit was with Simeon, and God had told Simeon that he would not die until he saw the One who would rescue people from their sin.**

That day, God's Spirit had led Simeon to the temple. **Simeon saw Jesus and picked Him up in his arms.** God's Spirit showed Simeon that Jesus was the promised Messiah. Simeon was so happy. He praised God and said, "Lord, you can let me die now. You kept Your promise, and I have seen the One who will save people from sin." **Simeon said that Jesus would save God's people, the Israelites, and Jesus would also save people from other nations.**

Mary and Joseph were amazed at what Simeon said about Jesus. Simeon blessed Mary and Joseph. He told Mary that being Jesus' mother would be a very good thing, but it would also be very hard. Some people would love Jesus, but others would hate Him. Things were going to happen that would make Mary very sad.

A woman named Anna was also at the temple. Anna was a prophetess, a female prophet. Anna's husband had died, and Anna was very old. She stayed at the temple and worshiped God all the time. She prayed and fasted. **Anna came up to Simeon, Jesus, Mary, and Joseph**

and she began to thank God. Anna talked about Jesus to people who were waiting for God to keep His promise to send a Savior. She told them the good news: the Savior was here!

Mary and Joseph finished dedicating Jesus and making sacrifices to God. They obeyed God's law. Then they went back home to Nazareth. Jesus grew up and was strong and healthy. He was wise, and God was happy with Him.

Christ Connection: Throughout the Old Testament, God promised the arrival of a king who would redeem God's people. When Jesus arrived, Simeon and Anna knew He was the promised Messiah. Today, we have faith that Jesus is God's Son. We can trust Jesus for our salvation, and like Simeon and Anna, we should share the good news.

Small Group OPENING

Session Title: Jesus Was Dedicated
Bible Passage: Luke 2:21-40
Big Picture Question: Why were Simeon and Anna waiting? Simeon and Anna were waiting for God to keep His promise to send Jesus to save them from their sins.
Key Passage: John 1:14
Unit Christ Connection: Old Testament prophecies looked forward to the birth of Christ. Jesus' roles as Son of God and Messiah are established.

Welcome time

Greet each kid as he or she arrives. Use this time to collect the offering, fill out attendance sheets, and help new kids connect to your group.

Ask kids to share about a time when they had to wait a very long time for something. What did they wait for? Was the wait worth it?

Activity page (5 minutes)

- "How Long?" activity page, 1 per kid
- pencils

Guide kids to complete the "How Long?" activity page. Offer assistance to kids who need help with subtraction. Talk about how long kids have to wait to meet some of these age requirements.

Say • Waiting for something can be hard. But if the event we are waiting for is wonderful, it is worth the wait.

Session starter (10 minutes)

Option 1: Going on a trip
Direct the kids to sit in a circle. Sit with them. Explain the game. Kids will take turns sharing an alphabetical item they would like to take on a trip. When a kid shares an item, he

must also repeat the items previously shared.

For example, start the game by saying, "I'm going on a trip, and I'm bringing an apple." The next kid will say an item that begins with the next letter of the alphabet, and then he will repeat previous items: "I'm going on a trip, and I'm bringing a baseball and an apple." The third kid will say, "I'm going on a trip, and I'm bringing a cookie, a baseball, and an apple."

Continue play until everyone has had a turn. To speed up the game, play in smaller groups. If a player struggles to remember a previous item, ask the group to remind her.

Say • In today's Bible story, Mary and Joseph took Jesus on a trip. I wonder what types of items they took.

Option 2: Set apart

- Allergy Alert (enhanced CD)
- small paper cups
- light corn syrup
- honey
- dish soap
- water
- vegetable oil
- rubbing alcohol
- large, clear jar
- marker

Prior to class, pour equal amounts of the following liquids into separate small paper cups: light corn syrup, honey, dish soap, water, vegetable oil, and rubbing alcohol. Label the cups according to their contents.

Display a large, clear jar. Ask the kids what they think these liquids will look like when you pour them in the jar.

Call for the liquids one at a time. They must be added in this order: honey, light corn syrup, dish soap, water, vegetable oil, and rubbing alcohol. As you pour, explain to kids what is happening. The liquids' densities (how close together the molecules are) will prevent the liquids from mixing. High-density liquid stays at the bottom, and low-density liquid floats at the top.

Say • Like these liquids were each separated, or set apart, someone in today's Bible story was set apart. His parents promised to dedicate Him to the Lord.

Transition to large group

Large Group LEADER

Session Title: Jesus Was Dedicated
Bible Passage: Luke 2:21-40
Big Picture Question: Why were Simeon and Anna waiting? Simeon and Anna were waiting for God to keep His promise to send Jesus to save them from their sins.
Key Passage: John 1:14
Unit Christ Connection: Old Testament prophecies looked forward to the birth of Christ. Jesus' roles as Son of God and Messiah are established.

Countdown

• countdown video

Show the countdown video as your kids arrive, and set it to end as large group time begins.

Introduce the session (3 minutes)

• camera

[Large Group Leader enters holding a camera and snapping photos while directing kids as if they are models.]

Leader • Look at me! Right at the camera! Beautiful! Just gorgeous! Now turn your heads to the left, chins up just a little … perfect!

Whew, being a photographer is hard work! There's so much to think about! You can't just push a button and expect to get a great photo. You have to hold the camera very still and focus on your subject. Sometimes you have to zoom in or out or move around to get just the right angle. Sometimes you have to wait for just the right moment. [*Hold up the camera again.*] Wait for it … there! Timing is very important.

I'm [*your name*], by the way. I'm glad you're back. I hope you'll stick with me and learn a little bit about photography and—best of all—the Bible!

Older Kids Bible Study Leader Guide
Unit 24 • Session 2

Timeline map (1 minute)

• Timeline Map

Point to each story on the timeline map as you review.

Leader • Let's look at our timeline map. Where are we now? Oh, here we are. Last week we heard the Bible story "Jesus Was Born." Do you remember, *Why was Jesus born? Jesus was born to be God's promised Savior.* After Jesus was born, when He was still very young, His mom and dad—Mary and Joseph—took Him to the temple to be dedicated. That's our Bible story today: "Jesus Was Dedicated."

Big picture question (1 minute)

• Bibles, 1 per kid

Leader • Mary, Joseph, and Jesus weren't the only people at the temple. The priest was there, and two people named Simeon and Anna were there too. Simeon and Anna were waiting for something. I wonder what. Actually, that's our big picture question today: *Why were Simeon and Anna waiting?* Listen to the Bible story to find out why they were waiting.

Guide kids to turn to Luke 2 in their Bibles.

Tell the Bible story (10 minutes)

• "Jesus Was Dedicated" video
• Bible Story Picture Slide or Poster
• Big Picture Question Slide or Poster

Open your Bible to Luke 2:21-40 and tell the Bible story in your own words, or show the Bible story video "Jesus Was Dedicated."

Leader • Now, who can answer our big picture question? *Why were Simeon and Anna waiting?* Yes! *Simeon and Anna were waiting for God to keep His promise to send Jesus to save them from their sins.* Let's say the big picture question and answer together. *Why were Simeon and Anna waiting? Simeon and Anna were waiting for God to keep His promise to send Jesus to save them from their sins.*

Shortly after Jesus was born, Mary and Joseph took Him to the temple to be dedicated. Mary and Joseph obeyed the law God gave to Moses. The law said that a firstborn son should be dedicated to the Lord. By dedicating Jesus, Mary and Joseph were showing that they knew Jesus did not belong to them; He belongs to God. They would raise Jesus to know, love, and serve God.

Simeon and Anna were at the temple when Mary, Joseph, and Jesus were there. How did they know that Jesus was the Savior, the promised Messiah? God revealed it to them. God's Spirit told Simeon that the wait was over. God had kept His promise to send Jesus to save people from their sin.

I have a question. Why do people need to be saved from their sin? Everyone sins, or disobeys God. We deserve to be punished for our sin, and the punishment for sin is death—eternal separation from God. But God loves us, and He sent Jesus to take the punishment for us. Jesus died the death we deserve, and then God raised Him from the dead. When we trust in Jesus, God forgives us for our sin, and we can be with Him forever.

The Gospel: God's Plan for Me (optional)

Using Scripture and the guide provided, explain to boys and girls how to become a Christian. Tell kids how they can respond, and provide counselors to speak with each kid individually. Guide counselors to use open-ended questions to allow kids to determine the direction of the conversation.

Encourage boys and girls to ask their parents, small group leaders, or other adults any questions they may have about becoming a Christian.

Older Kids Bible Study Leader Guide
Unit 24 • Session 2

Key passage (5 minutes)

- Key Passage Slide or Poster
- "Grace and Truth" song

Leader • Can anyone say our key passage from memory? Let's say it together using the motions we learned last week.

Guide kids to recite the verse using these motions with the key words: *Word*—palms together, then open like a book; *flesh*—hold hands in front of you and turn palms up and down to show your skin; *among*—hold palms up at your side and turn hips right to left; *seen/observed*—curl fingers around eyes like binoculars; *One and Only*—hold up one finger; *Father*—spread five fingers and touch thumb to forehead; *truth*—use hands to form a *T* shape.

Sing the key passage song "Grace and Truth."

Discussion starter video (4 minutes)

- "Unit 24 Session 2" discussion starter video

Leader • According to our big picture question and answer, ***Why were Simeon and Anna waiting? Simeon and Anna were waiting for God to keep His promise to send Jesus to save them from their sins.***

Remember, Mary and Joseph took Jesus to the temple because they wanted to obey God's law by dedicating their Son to the Lord. By dedicating Jesus, they showed that Jesus belongs to God, not them. They set Him apart for a special purpose. Check out this video.

Show the "Unit 24 Session 2" video.

Leader • Have you ever set anything apart? Maybe you kept your best toys or clothes for a special occasion, or you might have set some money aside for an event or special purchase.

Parents today sometimes dedicate their children to God. They commit to raising their children to know, love, and serve God.

If your church hosts dedication services for children,

discuss the details, such as what dedication means and how everyone in the church commits to helping children know, love, and serve God.

Sing (4 minutes)

• "In Jesus' Name" song

Leader • Who is ready to sing praises to God? Let me hear you clap and cheer when I raise my hand.

Raise your hand, and allow kids to clap and cheer. Then lower your hand.

Leader • Stand with me and let's sing our theme song.

Lead boys and girls to sing "In Jesus' Name."

Prayer (2 minutes)

Leader • *Why were Simeon and Anna waiting? Simeon and Anna were waiting for God to keep His promise to send Jesus to save them from their sins.* Waiting is worth it when you're waiting on God because you will never be disappointed. God always keeps His promises.

Close in prayer. Thank God for giving us His Word—the Bible—so we can learn about and know Jesus, the One who saves people from sin.

Dismiss to small groups

The Gospel: God's Plan for Me

Ask kids if they have ever heard the word *gospel*. Clarify that the word *gospel* means "good news." It is the message about Christ, the kingdom of God, and salvation. Use the following guide to share the gospel with kids.

God rules. Explain to kids that the Bible tells us God created everything, and He is in charge of everything. Invite a volunteer to read Genesis 1:1 from the Bible. Read Revelation 4:11 or Colossians 1:16-17 aloud and explain what these verses mean.

We sinned. Tell kids that since the time of Adam and Eve, everyone has chosen to disobey God. (Romans 3:23) The Bible calls this sin. Because God is holy, God cannot be around sin. Sin separates us from God and deserves God's punishment of death. (Romans 6:23)

God provided. Choose a child to read John 3:16 aloud. Say that God sent His Son, Jesus, the perfect solution to our sin problem, to rescue us from the punishment we deserve. It's something we, as sinners, could never earn on our own. Jesus alone saves us. Read and explain Ephesians 2:8-9.

Jesus gives. Share with kids that Jesus lived a perfect life, died on the cross for our sins, and rose again. Because Jesus gave up His life for us, we can be welcomed into God's family for eternity. This is the best gift ever! Read Romans 5:8; 2 Corinthians 5:21; or 1 Peter 3:18.

We respond. Tell kids that they can respond to Jesus. Read Romans 10:9-10,13. Review these aspects of our response: Believe in your heart that Jesus alone saves you through what He's already done on the cross. Repent, turning from self and sin to Jesus. Tell God and others that your faith is in Jesus.

Offer to talk with any child who is interested in responding to Jesus.

Small Group LEADER

Session Title: Jesus Was Dedicated
Bible Passage: Luke 2:21-40
Big Picture Question: Why were Simeon and Anna waiting? Simeon and Anna were waiting for God to keep His promise to send Jesus to save them from their sins.
Key Passage: John 1:14
Unit Christ Connection: Old Testament prophecies looked forward to the birth of Christ. Jesus' roles as Son of God and Messiah are established.

Key passage activity (5 minutes)

- Key Passage Poster
- craft sticks
- marker

Write words or phrases of the key passage on several craft sticks. Use enough sticks for each kid to have at least one.

Distribute the craft sticks. Instruct kids to work together to arrange them in the correct order. Then lead the group to read the key passage aloud. As time allows, mix up the sticks and play again.

Say • Great job, everyone. In today's Bible story, Mary and Joseph dedicated Jesus to show that He belongs to God. That means they wanted Jesus to do God's plan. In our key passage, John said that Jesus is the One and Only Son of God. Jesus is always obedient to His Father.

Bible story review & Bible skills (10 minutes)

- Bibles, 1 per kid
- Small Group Visual Pack
- large pieces of paper, 4
- crayons or markers

Help kids find Luke 2:21-40 in their Bibles. Show the timeline in the small group visual pack. Retell or review the Bible story in your own words, or use the bolded text of the Bible story script.

Form four groups of kids. Give each group a large piece of paper and crayons or markers. Assign each group a passage from the Bible story: Luke 2:22-24; Luke 2:25-32; Luke 2:33-35; Luke 2:36-38.

Instruct each group to read its assigned passage in the Bible. Then guide kids to work in their groups to illustrate the passage. After a few minutes, call kids to make finishing touches on their drawings. Then invite them to take turns retelling each part of the Bible story. If necessary, gently correct any misinformation.

Say • *Why were Simeon and Anna waiting? Simeon and Anna were waiting for God to keep His promise to send Jesus to save them from their sins.*

- Did God keep His promise? Yes. When Jesus arrived, Simeon and Anna knew He was the promised Messiah.

- Today, we have faith that Jesus is God's Son. We can trust Jesus for our salvation.

If you choose to review with boys and girls how to become a Christian, explain that kids are welcome to speak with you or another teacher if they have questions.

- **God rules.** God created and is in charge of everything. (Gen. 1:1; Rev. 4:11; Col. 1:16-17)

- **We sinned.** Since Adam and Eve, everyone has chosen to disobey God. (Rom. 3:23; 6:23)

- **God provided.** God sent His Son, Jesus, to rescue us from the punishment we deserve. (John 3:16; Eph. 2:8-9)

- **Jesus gives.** Jesus lived a perfect life, died on the cross for our sins, and rose again so we can be welcomed into God's family. (Rom. 5:8; 2 Cor. 5:21; 1 Pet. 3:18)

- **We respond.** Believe that Jesus alone saves you. Repent. Tell God that your faith is in Jesus. (Rom. 10:9-10,13)

Activity choice (10 minutes)

Option 1: My eyes have seen

Invite kids to play a guessing game. Choose one player to lead. The leader should pick something in the room that is visible to everyone. He should say, "My eyes have seen … " and then he should give a hint. For example, "My eyes have seen something that starts with the letter *P*." Or "My eyes have seen something orange."

Kids should try to guess what the leader has spotted. When a player guesses correctly, she gets to be the new leader. Make sure every kid has a turn to lead.

Say • *Why were Simeon and Anna waiting? Simeon and Anna were waiting for God to keep His promise to send Jesus to save them from their sins.*

• Did God keep His promise? Yes! What did Simeon say when he saw Jesus at the temple? Simeon said, "My eyes have seen Your salvation." Simeon saw Jesus, the One who would save people from sin.

Option 2: "God Will" cards

• large sheet of paper
• index cards
• markers
• hole punch
• binder rings or ribbon

List the following verses on a large sheet of paper and display it where everyone can see it: *Numbers 23:19*; *Psalm 89:34*; *Psalm 27:13-14*; *Psalm 32:8*; *Psalm 103:8*; *Psalm 145:9*; *Psalm 145:13*; *Isaiah 40:8*; *Isaiah 46:11*; *Romans 8:38-39*; *James 1:17*.

Supply markers and three or four index cards per kid. Remind kids that God always keeps His promises. Explain that the Bible is full of promises from God. Invite them to look up some of the promise passage in the Bible and write some of God's promises on their cards. Kids may copy the verse word for word, or they may paraphrase and list the reference. For example: *Nothing can separate us from God. (Romans 8:38-39)*

Assist kids in looking up verses. Provide hole punches for kids to punch a hole in the top left corner of each card. Demonstrate how to hold the cards together with a binder ring or length of ribbon.

Say • *Why were Simeon and Anna waiting? Simeon and Anna were waiting for God to keep His promise to send Jesus to save them from their sins.*

• God is faithful, and He always keeps His promises. The next time you find yourself waiting somewhere, read over these cards and remember the good promises God has for you.

Journal and prayer (5 minutes)

• pencils
• journals
• Bibles
• Journal Page, 1 per kid (enhanced CD)
• "Picture Puzzle" activity page, 1 per kid

Prompt each kid to write about a time he didn't keep a promise to someone or a time someone didn't keep a promise to him. How did he feel? How does he feel knowing that God always keeps His promises?

Say • Simeon and Anna waited for God to keep His promise, and God did. God sent Jesus to save people from their sins.

Invite kids to share prayer requests. Close the group in prayer or allow a couple volunteers to close the group in prayer. Pray: "God, thank You for always keeping Your promises. The news that Jesus came to save people from sin is such good news. We confess that we do not always keep our promises, but You, Lord, are faithful. Help us trust in Jesus for our salvation."

As time allows, lead kids to complete the activity page "Picture Puzzle."

Leader BIBLE STUDY

The Book of Luke records just two narratives about Jesus' childhood: His dedication (Luke 2:21-40) and His time at the temple when He was 12 years old (Luke 2:41-52). Both stories set the stage for Jesus' ministry on earth as an adult.

Mary and Joseph were faithful Jews. They had dedicated the baby Jesus according to the law of Moses, and they traveled to Jerusalem each year to celebrate Passover. God had commanded the men to appear before Him three times a year to observe certain festivals. (See Deut. 16:16.) Once a year, those who followed God's law would travel to Jerusalem, often in large groups.

In Bible times, a Jewish boy became a man around age 12. His father would train him to take on all the responsibilities of adulthood, social and spiritual. Joseph was a carpenter, and he likely trained Jesus in his trade. When Mary and Joseph went to Jerusalem, Joseph might have taken Jesus around the city to teach Him the significance of the temple and explain the purpose of the Passover feast.

Jesus' parents started the journey back home after the feast. They assumed Jesus was among their traveling companions, but He wasn't. Jesus had stayed behind at the temple. Mary and Joseph traveled for a day before they noticed Jesus was missing. They went back to Jerusalem and found Him at the temple.

Jesus said to them: "Didn't you know that I had to be in My Father's house?" Mary and Joseph did not understand Jesus' words. But Jesus is God's Son, and it was necessary that He honor His true Father. In all this, Jesus did not sin.

The Bible does not give many details about Jesus' childhood, but we do know that as Jesus got older, He grew in wisdom and stature, and in favor with God and with people. Jesus carried out God's plan to reconcile the world to Himself. (2 Cor. 5:19)

Older Kids BIBLE STUDY OVERVIEW

Session Title: Jesus at the Temple
Bible Passage: Luke 2:41-52
Big Picture Question: Why was Jesus' visit to the temple important?
Jesus showed that He is God's Son and that He came to do God's will.
Key Passage: John 1:14
Unit Christ Connection: Old Testament prophecies looked forward to the birth of Christ. Jesus' roles as Son of God and Messiah are established.

Small Group Opening

Welcome time ....Page 166
Activity page (5 minutes)..Page 166
Session starter (10 minutes) ....Page 166

Large Group Leader

Countdown ....Page 168
Introduce the session (3 minutes) ....Page 168
Timeline map (1 minute)...Page 169
Big picture question (1 minute) ....Page 169
Tell the Bible story (10 minutes) ....Page 169
The Gospel: God's Plan for Me (optional) ....Page 170
Key passage (5 minutes) ....Page 171
Discussion starter video (5 minutes)................................Page 171
Sing (3 minutes)..Page 171
Prayer (2 minutes)..Page 172

Small Group Leader

Key passage activity (5 minutes) ....Page 174
Bible story review & Bible skills (10 minutes)..................Page 174
Activity choice (10 minutes)..Page 176
Journal and prayer (5 minutes) ....Page 177

The BIBLE STORY

Jesus at the Temple
Luke 2:41-52

Every year, Jesus' parents traveled to Jerusalem for the Passover Festival. Passover was the biggest holiday for the Jewish people. Many people would travel to Jerusalem **to celebrate and remember when God saved His people from slavery in Egypt.**

When Jesus was 12 years old, Jesus, Mary, and Joseph went to Jerusalem together. When it was time to go home, Mary and Joseph began traveling to Nazareth with a large group of people. They did not notice that Jesus was not with them; they thought He was among the group of travelers. But Jesus was not with the group. **He had stayed behind in Jerusalem.**

Mary, Joseph, and the other travelers had been walking for a whole day when they began to look for Jesus. They looked among their relatives and friends, but **they could not find Him.**

So Mary and Joseph went back to Jerusalem to look for Jesus. They searched everywhere for Him, but they could not find Him. The city was so big, and Jesus was just a boy.

Finally, they found Him. Jesus was in the temple complex, sitting among the teachers. Jesus was listening to the teachers and asking them questions. Everyone who heard Jesus could hardly believe how much Jesus understood.

When Jesus' parents saw Him, they were surprised. **Mary said, "Son, why have You done this? Your father and I were worried. We've been looking everywhere for You."**

"Why were you looking for Me?" Jesus asked them. "Didn't you know that I had to be in My Father's house?"

But Mary and Joseph did not understand what Jesus was talking about. **Then Jesus went back to Nazareth with Mary and Joseph, and He was obedient to them.** Mary remembered all of these things.

Jesus grew taller and wiser. God was pleased with Him, and so was everyone who knew Him.

Christ Connection: Jesus went to the temple to worship. He is God's Son, and He came to do God's work. Jesus taught people, suffered, died on the cross for our sins, and rose from the dead so that we too can worship God.

Small Group OPENING

Session Title: Jesus at the Temple
Bible Passage: Luke 2:41-52
Big Picture Question: Why was Jesus' visit to the temple important?
Jesus showed that He is God's Son and that He came to do God's will.
Key Passage: John 1:14
Unit Christ Connection: Old Testament prophecies looked forward to the birth of Christ. Jesus' roles as Son of God and Messiah are established.

Welcome time

Greet each kid as he or she arrives. Use this time to collect the offering, fill out attendance sheets, and help new kids connect to your group. Ask each kid to talk about something she has lost. How did she feel? Did she ever find the item?

Activity page (5 minutes)

- "Searching Scene" activity page, 1 per kid
- pencils

Invite kids to work in pairs or small groups to complete the "Searching Scene" activity page. Challenge kids to find and circle all of the birds in the park scene. Fifteen birds are hidden in the picture.

Say • How good are your searching skills? Losing something I love makes me feel scared or sad. I look everywhere for it! When I find it, I feel so relieved.

Session starter (10 minutes)

Option 1: Amazing accomplishments
Invite a couple kids to share their greatest accomplishments. Explain that you will read a list of accomplishments. If kids think a 12-year-old accomplished the feat, they should clap and cheer. If not, they should remain silent.

1. A 12-year-old boy from Oregon graduated from a

college in Chicago.

2. A 12-year-old boy from India was accepted into medical school.

3. A 12-year-old girl from China had her paintings appear in worldwide museum exhibits.

4. A 12-year-old boy from Pennsylvania was nominated for the Nobel Peace Prize.

5. A 12-year-old boy from France could read six languages.

6. A 12-year-old boy from Taiwan was accepted into an important music school in England.

Say • All of these accomplishments were actually achieved by 12-year-olds! Today we are going to hear a story from the Bible about something Jesus did when He was 12 years old. What Jesus did amazed the adults who saw Him!

Option 2: Human obstacle course

Tip: Make sure kids choose stances that are appropriate for their style of clothing.

Invite the kids to form a human obstacle course by standing throughout the room. Each kid may stand with his feet wide apart, crouch on his hands and knees, or stand with his arms outstretched like the letter *T*. At each obstacle, the course runner should pass over, under, or around the obstacle.

Guide the first player through the course. When she finishes, instruct her to take the place of an obstacle and let another kid run the course.

Say • Moving around obstacles can be hard! It's much harder than just walking without obstacles. In today's Bible story, Mary and Joseph moved quickly through a crowd because they were looking for Jesus. Do you think they found Him? We will soon find out!

Transition to large group

God's Plan is Jesus

Large Group LEADER

Session Title: Jesus at the Temple
Bible Passage: Luke 2:41-52
Big Picture Question: Why was Jesus' visit to the temple important?
Jesus showed that He is God's Son and that He came to do God's will.
Key Passage: John 1:14
Unit Christ Connection: Old Testament prophecies looked forward to the birth of Christ. Jesus' roles as Son of God and Messiah are established.

Countdown

• countdown video

Show the countdown video as your kids arrive, and set it to end as large group time begins.

Introduce the session (3 minutes)

• photo album

[Large Group Leader enters carrying a photo album.]
Leader • Welcome back, everyone! In case you forgot, I'm [*your name*], and we have been learning about photography. We already learned that the first photos were made nearly 200 years ago! And photography can be tricky. It's an art, and if you want to get a really good photo, you have to learn all about your camera, different lighting and angles … all kinds of things.

Now I want to explain another important thing about taking a photo: the subject. What makes a photo interesting is often the very thing you are taking a photo of! Imagine you're taking a photo of a person. How should that person stand? Should she look directly at the camera or off into the distance? In what location will you take the photo? These are all very important things to think about!

That reminds me, are you ready to hear another story from the Bible? The Bible is God's Word, and everything in it is true; these stories really happened! Today's story is about our subject—Jesus—in a special location—the temple—for a very important reason!

Timeline map (1 minute)

• Timeline Map

Remember to point to each story—"Jesus Was Born" and "Jesus Was Dedicated"—on the timeline as you review.

Leader • Before we get to the Bible story, let's review our timeline map. So far we have learned about Jesus' birth and dedication. Who remembers which books of the Bible tell about Jesus' life? (*the Gospels: Matthew, Mark, Luke, John*) Who can tell me, **Why was Jesus born?** Right! *Jesus was born to be God's promised Savior.* When Jesus was still young, His parents took Him to the temple to dedicate Him to God. Simeon and Anna were waiting at the temple. Do you remember, **Why were Simeon and Anna waiting?** Right again. *Simeon and Anna were waiting for God to keep His promise to send Jesus to save them from their sins.*

Big picture question (1 minute)

Leader • That leads me to our big picture question. Our big picture question is, **Why was Jesus' visit to the temple important?** That is a very good question. I'm sure Jesus had a reason for going to the temple. Let's listen to today's Bible story to see if we can find the answer to our big picture question.

Tell the Bible story (10 minutes)

• "Jesus at the Temple" video
• Bibles, 1 per kid
• Bible Story Picture Slide or Poster
• Big Picture Question Slide or Poster

Open your Bible to Luke 2:41-52 and tell the Bible story in your own words, or show the video "Jesus at the Temple."

Leader • Mary and Joseph went to Jerusalem every year. The Jewish people celebrated Passover to remember the first Passover when God rescued His people from slavery in Egypt. When Jesus was 12 years old, He went to Jerusalem with Mary and Joseph. After the celebration, a whole crowd of people headed home. The people in the crowd were Mary and Joseph's friends and relatives. Mary and Joseph thought Jesus was somewhere in the crowd, but He wasn't. After a day of traveling, they realized Jesus wasn't with them.

Imagine how Mary and Joseph must have felt! They hurried back to Jerusalem, retracing their steps. Finally, they found Jesus at the temple. Can anyone tell me what Jesus was doing at the temple? Jesus was listening to the teachers and asking them questions. Jesus said to Mary and Joseph, "Didn't you know that I had to be in My Father's house?"

What did He mean? Remember, Jesus is God's Son! God gave Jesus earthly parents, but Jesus was born to be the Savior of the world! He came to do God's will. ***Why was Jesus' visit to the temple important? Jesus showed that He is God's Son and that He came to do God's will.*** Say the big picture question and answer with me. ***Why was Jesus' visit to the temple important? Jesus showed that He is God's Son and that He came to do God's will.*** While Jesus was on earth, He taught people, suffered, died on the cross for our sins, and rose from the dead.

The Gospel: God's Plan for Me (optional)

Using Scripture and the guide provided, explain to boys and girls how to become a Christian. Tell kids how they can respond, and provide counselors to speak with each kid individually. Guide counselors to use open-ended questions to allow kids to determine the direction of the conversation.

Encourage boys and girls to ask their parents, small

group leaders, or other adults any questions they may have about becoming a Christian.

Key passage (5 minutes)

• Key Passage Slide or Poster
• "Grace and Truth" song

Leader • Let's say our key passage together. This is interesting. John wrote in his Gospel that Jesus (the Word) came and lived among us. When did that happen? (*When Jesus was born.*) John also wrote that Jesus is the One and Only Son from the Father. Can anyone tell me who the Father is? (*God*) Yes! Jesus is the Son of God. Lead kids in singing "Grace and Truth."

Discussion starter video (5 minutes)

• "Unit 24 Session 3" discussion starter video

Leader • Raise your hand if you've ever lost something. Did you ever find it? Where?

Allow kids to share their experiences. Then show the "Unit 24 Session 3" video.

Leader • Finding something I've lost makes me feel so happy. Have you ever found something right where it belonged? Mary and Joseph searched for Jesus, and they finally found Him in the temple. Jesus said that He had to be in His Father's house.

Why was Jesus' visit to the temple important? Jesus showed that He is God's Son and that He came to do God's will.

Sing (3 minutes)

• "In Jesus' Name" song

Leader • Jesus came to do God's work. He didn't have His own plans about what His life would be like. Jesus was completely obedient to God and God's plan for His life, even though that plan was not easy. Jesus taught people, suffered, died on the cross for our sins, and rose again. Because of Him, we can worship God. Let's worship Him now. Sing our theme song with me.

Lead boys and girls to sing "In Jesus' Name."

Prayer (2 minutes)

Leader • Thanks for being here, everyone. I hope you'll
remember this week's photography tip: Think about the
subject! (The subject, of course, is what you're taking a
picture of!) I hope you also learned a lot about the subject
of today's Bible story: Jesus. Jesus is actually the subject
of the whole Bible! The Bible is all about God's plan to
bring sinners back to Himself through His Son, Jesus.

Before you go to your small groups, I'm going to pray.

Close in prayer. Thank God for sending His Son, Jesus, to
do His will. Pray that God will lead kids to trust in Jesus as
their Lord and Savior.

Dismiss to small groups

The Gospel: God's Plan for Me

Ask kids if they have ever heard the word *gospel*. Clarify that the word *gospel* means "good news." It is the message about Christ, the kingdom of God, and salvation. Use the following guide to share the gospel with kids.

God rules. Explain to kids that the Bible tells us God created everything, and He is in charge of everything. Invite a volunteer to read Genesis 1:1 from the Bible. Read Revelation 4:11 or Colossians 1:16-17 aloud and explain what these verses mean.

We sinned. Tell kids that since the time of Adam and Eve, everyone has chosen to disobey God. (Romans 3:23) The Bible calls this sin. Because God is holy, God cannot be around sin. Sin separates us from God and deserves God's punishment of death. (Romans 6:23)

God provided. Choose a child to read John 3:16 aloud. Say that God sent His Son, Jesus, the perfect solution to our sin problem, to rescue us from the punishment we deserve. It's something we, as sinners, could never earn on our own. Jesus alone saves us. Read and explain Ephesians 2:8-9.

Jesus gives. Share with kids that Jesus lived a perfect life, died on the cross for our sins, and rose again. Because Jesus gave up His life for us, we can be welcomed into God's family for eternity. This is the best gift ever! Read Romans 5:8; 2 Corinthians 5:21; or 1 Peter 3:18.

We respond. Tell kids that they can respond to Jesus. Read Romans 10:9-10,13. Review these aspects of our response: Believe in your heart that Jesus alone saves you through what He's already done on the cross. Repent, turning from self and sin to Jesus. Tell God and others that your faith is in Jesus.

Offer to talk with any child who is interested in responding to Jesus.

Small Group LEADER

Session Title: Jesus at the Temple
Bible Passage: Luke 2:41-52
Big Picture Question: Why was Jesus' visit to the temple important?
Jesus showed that He is God's Son and that He came to do God's will.
Key Passage: John 1:14
Unit Christ Connection: Old Testament prophecies looked forward to the birth of Christ. Jesus' roles as Son of God and Messiah are established.

Key passage activity (5 minutes)

• Key Passage Poster

Direct kids to sit in a circle. Invite them to play an echo game to practice the key passage. First, lead everyone to say the key passage together. Then choose one kid to begin. The first kid will say the first word of the passage. The next kid will echo the first word and then say the second word. The third kid will echo the second word and say the third word. Continue until kids recite the entire key passage.

Say • Great job, everyone. Our key passage reminds me of what we learned in today's Bible story. Jesus is the One and Only Son from the Father. Do you remember, *Why was Jesus' visit to the temple important? Jesus showed that He is God's Son and that He came to do God's will.*

Bible story review & Bible skills (10 minutes)

• Bibles, 1 per kid
• Small Group Visual Pack

Option: Retell or review the Bible story using the bolded text of the Bible story script.

Review the timeline in the small group visual pack. Then help kids find Luke 2:41-52 in their Bibles. Invite volunteers to take turns reading two verses at a time until they read the entire passage. Ask the following review questions about the story. Encourage the kids to look over the story in their Bibles to find the answers. If a kid knows the answer, he should raise his hand. Allow time for several kids to raise their hands before calling on one of them to answer.

Say • How often did Mary and Joseph go to Jerusalem? (*every year, Luke 2:41*)

• How old was Jesus when He went to Jerusalem with His parents? (*12 years old, Luke 2:42*)

• How many days did Jesus' parents travel before they realized Jesus wasn't with them? (*one, Luke 2:44*)

• How many days did Mary and Joseph search for Jesus? (*three days, Luke 2:46*)

• Where did Mary and Joseph find Jesus? (*in the temple, Luke 2:46*)

• What was Jesus doing in the temple? (*sitting among the teachers, listening to them and asking them questions; Luke 2:46*)

• Where did Jesus say He had to be? (*in His Father's house, Luke 2:49*)

• ***Why was Jesus' visit to the temple important? Jesus showed that He is God's Son and that He came to do God's will.***

• Did Jesus disobey His parents when He stayed at the temple? (*No, Jesus never sinned.*) Jesus did what was right. He was in the temple—His Father's house—because He is God's Son. Jesus showed that He is God's Son and that He came to do God's will. He came to save people from their sins.

If you choose to review with boys and girls how to become a Christian, explain that kids are welcome to speak with you or another teacher if they have questions.

• **God rules.** God created and is in charge of everything. (Gen. 1:1; Rev. 4:11; Col. 1:16-17)

• **We sinned.** Since Adam and Eve, everyone has chosen to disobey God. (Rom. 3:23; 6:23)

- **God provided.** God sent His Son, Jesus, to rescue us from the punishment we deserve. (John 3:16; Eph. 2:8-9)
- **Jesus gives.** Jesus lived a perfect life, died on the cross for our sins, and rose again so we can be welcomed into God's family. (Rom. 5:8; 2 Cor. 5:21; 1 Pet. 3:18)
- **We respond.** Believe that Jesus alone saves you. Repent. Tell God that your faith is in Jesus. (Rom. 10:9-10,13)

Activity choice (10 minutes)

• index cards, 1 per kid
• marker

Option 1: Let's ask questions

To prepare, write various nouns on separate index cards. Include people, places, and things. (Examples: Abraham Lincoln, New York, kite) Make one card for each kid. Form groups of three or four kids. Give each kid a card. Invite kids to take turns answering questions about their person, place, or thing. Kids should ask yes or no questions to try figure out what the noun is. Suggestions: Can you eat it? Is it a famous person? Is the place in America?

Say • Asking questions is a great way to get answers and learn new things. Jesus' parents found Him in the temple asking and answering questions.

• *Why was Jesus' visit to the temple important? Jesus showed that He is God's Son and that He came to do God's will.*

Option 2: My Father's house

• blindfold

Choose one volunteer to be the target. Lead him to practice saying his line: "Here I am!"

Choose another volunteer to be a searcher. Blindfold the searcher and lead her to practice her line: "Where are you?"

Older Kids Bible Study Leader Guide
Unit 24 • Session 3

Guide the rest of the class to spread out throughout the room. Explain the game: The searcher is trying to locate the target. The target must stay in one spot, but the other kids (obstacles) may move carefully around the room. Kids should clap or snap their fingers so the searcher can detect the obstacles. Supervise for safety.

As the searcher moves around, she should call out, "Where are you?" The target must respond, "Here I am!" The searcher should respond to the target's voice to locate him. When the searcher locates the target, choose new volunteers to be the searcher and target. Remaining kids will be obstacles.

Say • Jesus grew and worked with His father Joseph. God had chosen Joseph to be Jesus' earthly father, but Jesus' true Father is God. Even at a young age, Jesus understood that He is God's Son. He knew what was most important. That is why He said, "Why were you searching for Me? Didn't you know that I had to be in My Father's house?"

Journal and prayer (5 minutes)

• pencils
• journals
• Bibles
• Journal Page, 1 per kid (enhanced CD)
• "Looking for Jesus" activity page, 1 per kid

Remind kids that asking questions is one way to find out more about something. Encourage kids to write on their journal pages some questions they might have about God, Jesus, or the Bible. Encourage them to seek answers to their questions by talking with a teacher, parent, or church leader.

Say • *Why was Jesus' visit to the temple important? Jesus showed that He is God's Son and that He came to do God's will.*

Invite kids to share prayer requests. Close the group in prayer. As time allows, lead kids to complete the activity page "Looking for Jesus."

Leader BIBLE STUDY

Zechariah's son, John, lived in the wilderness. John's ministry began when God's word came to him, and he began preaching near the Jordan River. John worked to get the people ready for the coming of Jesus, fulfilling the Old Testament prophecy, "A voice of one crying out: Prepare the way of the Lord in the wilderness" (Isa. 40:3).

John called the people to repent of their sins, and he baptized them in the Jordan River. John also instructed the people on right living. (See Luke 3:10-14.) Some of the people suspected that John might be the Messiah, but John insisted, "One is coming who is more powerful than I" (Luke 3:16).

Jesus came from Galilee to be baptized by John at the Jordan River. Wait a second. John was calling people to a baptism of repentance. Who needs to repent? Sinners. But we know Jesus never sinned. (See Heb. 4:15; 2 Cor. 5:21.) So why did Jesus come to be baptized? John was right when he said, "I need to be baptized by You, and yet You come to me?" (Matt. 3:14).

Commentators' ideas vary about why Jesus was baptized. Perhaps He was affirming John's work. Maybe He was identifying with sinners or showing them how they would be saved—through His death, burial, and resurrection. Jesus answered John, "Allow it for now, because this is the way for us to fulfill all righteousness" (Matt. 3:15).

In the Book of Acts, the apostle Paul said, "John baptized with a baptism of repentance, telling the people that they should believe in the One who would come after him, that is, in Jesus" (Acts 19:4). John's baptism signaled the coming of the Holy Spirit. Christian baptism signals that the Spirit has come. Baptism reminds us that when we trust in Jesus, we die to sin and come into a new way of life—a life lived for Jesus. (See Rom. 6:3-4.)

Older Kids BIBLE STUDY OVERVIEW

Session Title: Jesus Was Baptized
Bible Passage: Matthew 3:13-17; Mark 1:1-11; Luke 3:21-22;
John 1:19-34
Big Picture Question: What does Jesus' baptism remind us of? Jesus'
baptism reminds us of His death and resurrection.
Key Passage: John 1:14
Unit Christ Connection: Old Testament prophecies looked forward to the
birth of Christ. Jesus' roles as Son of God and Messiah are established.

Small Group Opening

Welcome time ....Page 182
Activity page (5 minutes)..Page 182
Session starter (10 minutes) ....Page 182

Large Group Leader

Countdown..Page 184
Introduce the session (3 minutes) ....Page 184
Timeline map (2 minutes)..Page 185
Big picture question (1 minute) ....Page 185
Tell the Bible story (10 minutes) ....Page 185
The Gospel: God's Plan for Me (optional) ....Page 186
Key passage (5 minutes) ....Page 187
Discussion starter video (4 minutes)..................................Page 187
Sing (3 minutes)..Page 187
Prayer (2 minutes)...Page 188

Small Group Leader

Key passage activity (5 minutes) ....Page 190
Bible story review & Bible skills (10 minutes)....................Page 190
Activity choice (10 minutes)...Page 192
Journal and prayer (5 minutes) ....Page 193

The BIBLE STORY

Jesus Was Baptized

Matthew 3:13-17; Mark 1:1-11; Luke 3:21-22; John 1:19-34

John the Baptist lived in the wilderness. He wore camel's hair and a leather belt around his waist. He ate locusts and wild honey. **When John was an adult, he began speaking to the people around him. "Repent and be baptized, for God's kingdom is almost here," he said.**

Some of the people asked John, "Who are you?"

John said, "I am not the Messiah." John also said he wasn't Elijah, and he wasn't the Prophet.

"Who are you, then?" the people asked.

John said that he was the person Isaiah the prophet was talking about when he said, "There is someone shouting in the wilderness. He says, 'Prepare the way for the Lord; make His paths straight!'"

John was born with a very important job. He was supposed to get people ready for Jesus, God's promised Messiah.

People started to repent; they turned away from their sins and turned to God for forgiveness. Then John baptized them in the Jordan River. Baptism was a picture that the people's sins had been washed away. **John preached: "Someone more powerful than I will come after me. I am not worthy to bend down and untie His sandals."**

Then John said, "I baptize you with water, but He will baptize you with the Holy Spirit."

By this time, Jesus was an adult. He was in Galilee, and He left to see John the Baptist. **John was at the Jordan River, and Jesus came up to him. When John saw Jesus, he said, "Here is the Lamb of God, who takes away the sin of the world!"**

Jesus told John that He wanted to be baptized. John the Baptist didn't think he should baptize Jesus, and he tried to stop Him.

"I need You to baptize me," John said. "Why do you want me to baptize you?" John was confused because he baptized people who confessed their sins. Jesus never sinned!

Jesus said, "Allow me to be baptized. God says this is right." So John agreed, and he baptized Jesus.

Jesus immediately went up from the water. Suddenly, the heavens opened for Jesus, and He saw God's Spirit coming down on Him. The Spirit was like a dove. And a voice came from heaven. "This is My Son," the voice said. "I love Him, and I am very pleased with Him!"

Christ Connection: Jesus never sinned, but He was baptized like sinners are baptized. Baptism reminds us of Jesus' death and resurrection. It reminds us that when we trust in Jesus, we turn from sin and start a new life—a life lived for Jesus.

Small Group OPENING

Session Title: Jesus Was Baptized
Bible Passage: Matthew 3:13-17; Mark 1:1-11; Luke 3:21-22;
  John 1:19-34
Big Picture Question: What does Jesus' baptism remind us of? Jesus'
  baptism reminds us of His death and resurrection.
Key Passage: John 1:14
Unit Christ Connection: Old Testament prophecies looked forward to the
  birth of Christ. Jesus' roles as Son of God and Messiah are established.

Welcome time

Greet each kid as he or she arrives. Use this time to collect
the offering, fill out attendance sheets, and help new kids
connect to your group. Ask each kid to share whether she
would rather live under the sea or on the moon. Encourage
kids to explain their choices.

Activity page (5 minutes)

- "Air, Land, or Sea"
  activity page,
  1 per kid
- pencils

Instruct kids to complete the activity page "Air, Land,
or Sea." Kids should identify each animal's appropriate
environment. Invite kids to discuss their choices. Ask kids
which they like best: flying in the air, walking on the land,
or swimming in the water.

Say • When Jesus started His ministry on earth, He went
  into the water and was baptized.

Session starter (10 minutes)

Option 1: Fit to tie

- shoes with laces,
  1 per 2 kids

Guide kids to work in pairs. Give each pair of kids one shoe
with laces, or allow the pair to use one of their own shoes.
Instruct kids to begin with the shoelaces untied. When you

say go, kids should work together to tie the shoe using their non-dominant hands: kids who are right-handed should use their left hands, and kids who are left-handed should use their right hands.

Challenge kids to see how quickly they can tie the shoe.

Say • In Jesus' day, people often wore sandals to protect their feet. Some of the sandals had laces that were used to keep the sandals on a person's feet.

• In today's Bible story, John the Baptist said that he was not worthy to untie Jesus' sandals. Listen closely during large group to find out why.

Option 2: River crossing

• masking tape or painter's tape
• paper plates, 1 per kid

Mark a river on the floor by positioning tape lines about 10 feet apart. Give each kid a paper plate to use as a stepping stone. Each stone must be in contact with at least one person at all times. If the stepping stone loses contact, it "sinks" to the bottom of the river. (Pick up the stone and set it aside.) Challenge kids to use the stones to move the entire group across the river. If anyone falls into the river (touches the floor), the group must begin again.

Say • Rivers have long been an important source of water for people groups and cities. Cities were often built near rivers, lakes, or seas so the people would have a water supply.

• During Jesus' life on earth, the Jordan River ran from a mountain in Galilee, through the Sea of Galilee, and down to the Dead Sea in Judea. The Jordan River is where John the Baptist was baptizing people. Today we are going to hear the story about how Jesus was baptized in the Jordan River.

Transition to large group

Large Group LEADER

Session Title: Jesus Was Baptized
Bible Passage: Matthew 3:13-17; Mark 1:1-11; Luke 3:21-22;
John 1:19-34
Big Picture Question: What does Jesus' baptism remind us of? Jesus'
baptism reminds us of His death and resurrection.
Key Passage: John 1:14
Unit Christ Connection: Old Testament prophecies looked forward to the
birth of Christ. Jesus' roles as Son of God and Messiah are established.

Countdown

• countdown video

Show the countdown video as your kids arrive, and set it to
end as large group time begins.

Introduce the session (3 minutes)

• color photo
• black and white
  photo

*[Large Group Leader enters carrying a color photo and a
black and white photo.]*

Leader •Hello, everyone! Welcome back! It's so good
to see you. I'm [*your name*], and we've been learning
all about photography. Today's technology makes
photography accessible for everyone!

I wanted to show you these photos. What's the
difference? Yes! This photo is in color, and this one is in
black and white. Black and white photos are neat. I think
they make photos look old. But I really love color photos.
They can really make a subject come to life.

Oh, hey, are you ready for today's Bible story? It's
about the start of Jesus' ministry on earth. As you listen
to the Bible story today, think about the things you would
have heard, seen, smelled, felt, or tasted if you were
actually there. This Bible story can come to life!

Timeline map (2 minutes)

• Timeline Map

As you review the previous stories, point to each Bible story picture on the timeline map.

Leader • Here is our timeline map. The first story we heard was "Jesus Was Born." Do you remember why Jesus was born? *Jesus was born to be God's promised Savior.* Then Mary and Joseph took Jesus to the temple to be dedicated. Simeon and Anna were waiting at the temple. *Why were Simeon and Anna waiting? They were waiting for God to keep His promise to send Jesus to save them from their sins.* Then, when Jesus was 12, He visited the temple again. *Jesus' visit to the temple was important because Jesus showed that He is God's Son and that He came to do God's will.*

Big picture question (1 minute)

Leader • Today's Bible story is called "Jesus Was Baptized." The challenge today is to listen carefully to the Bible story and see if you can figure out the answer to our big picture question! Our big picture question is, *What does Jesus' baptism remind us of?* Interesting. Now that is something to think about.

Tell the Bible story (10 minutes)

• "Jesus Was Baptized" video
• Bibles
• Bible Story Picture Slide or Poster
• Big Picture Question Slide or Poster

Open your Bible to Matthew 3:13-17 and tell the Bible story in your own words, or show the Bible story video "Jesus Was Baptized."

Leader • God chose John the Baptist to be a messenger ahead of Jesus. John's job was to get people ready for Jesus. John told people that Jesus was coming. He told them to repent and be baptized. *Repent* means to be sorry for your sin, to turn away from your sin, and to turn toward God. John baptized people in the Jordan River as a picture that their sins had been washed away. Do you think the river had a smell? Was the water cold? Maybe John felt the warm sun on his skin.

While John was baptizing, Jesus came to the river. Jesus told John that He wanted to be baptized. John was confused. Imagine the look on his face. He had been baptizing people who confessed their sins. But Jesus never sinned. Jesus said, "Allow it. God says this is the right thing to do." So John baptized Jesus.

When Jesus came out of the water, the heavens opened and God's Spirit came down like a dove. Think about the sound of water dripping off of Jesus' body. Then a voice came from heaven. God the Father said, "This is My Son. I love Him, and I am very pleased with Him."

Jesus never sinned, but He was baptized like sinners are baptized. Baptism reminds us of Jesus' death and resurrection. It reminds us that when we trust in Jesus, we turn from sin and start a new life—a life lived for Jesus.

I think that's the answer to our big picture question. *What does Jesus' baptism remind us of? Jesus' baptism reminds us of His death and resurrection.* Are you ready to say it with me? OK! *What does Jesus' baptism remind us of? Jesus' baptism reminds us of His death and resurrection.*

That's great. Jesus died on the cross for our sin. After three days, God raised Him from the dead. Baptism today is a symbol. It reminds us of something greater than just being brought into and out of water. It reminds us of Jesus and what He did to save people from sin.

The Gospel: God's Plan for Me (optional)

Using Scripture and the guide provided, explain to boys and girls how to become a Christian. Tell kids how they can respond, and provide counselors to speak with each kid individually. Encourage boys and girls to ask their parents, small group leaders, or other adults any questions they may have about becoming a Christian.

Key passage (5 minutes)

• Key Passage Slide or Poster
• "Grace and Truth" song

Leader •Can anyone tell me who our key passage is about? Yes! It's about Jesus. When Jesus was born, He came to live among us. His life showed that He is God's Son. Read our key passage with me.

Lead kids to read the key passage together. Then cover the key passage poster and guide kids to recite the key passage from memory. Instruct kids to alternate standing and crouching as they say each word.

Sing "Grace and Truth."

Discussion starter video (4 minutes)

• "Unit 24 Session 4" discussion starter video

Leader • *What does Jesus' baptism remind us of? Jesus' baptism reminds us of His death and resurrection.* Believers are baptized today as a picture showing they trust in Jesus as Lord and Savior. Where are some of the places a person can be baptized? Check out this video.

Show the "Unit 24 Session 4" video.

Leader • Have any of you ever been baptized?

Allow kids to share their experiences. Emphasize that baptism comes after a person trusts in Jesus. Announce that you will be available at the end of class to talk with anyone who has questions about baptism.

Sing (3 minutes)

• "In Jesus' Name" song

Leader •Remember, Jesus never sinned. When we repent and trust in Jesus as Lord and Savior, we can be baptized to show others that we know and love Jesus.

Jesus' baptism reminds us of His death and resurrection. Because Jesus died for our sins and God raised Him from the dead, we can be forgiven for our sins. Let's praise God for sending Jesus to rescue us from sin.

Lead boys and girls to sing "In Jesus' Name."

Prayer (2 minutes)

Leader • Thank you for being here today. Good job imagining what it would have been like if you had been there with John at the Jordan River: the warm sun on your skin, the sound of the water, the smells, and the confused or surprised looks.

Before you move to your small groups to learn more about Jesus' baptism, I'm going to pray.

Pray, thanking God for Jesus, who died on the cross for our sin and was raised from the dead. Pray that kids who are believers will follow Jesus' example of baptism if they haven't already.

Dismiss to small groups

The Gospel: God's Plan for Me

Ask kids if they have ever heard the word *gospel*. Clarify that the word *gospel* means "good news." It is the message about Christ, the kingdom of God, and salvation. Use the following guide to share the gospel with kids.

God rules. Explain to kids that the Bible tells us God created everything, and He is in charge of everything. Invite a volunteer to read Genesis 1:1 from the Bible. Read Revelation 4:11 or Colossians 1:16-17 aloud and explain what these verses mean.

We sinned. Tell kids that since the time of Adam and Eve, everyone has chosen to disobey God. (Romans 3:23) The Bible calls this sin. Because God is holy, God cannot be around sin. Sin separates us from God and deserves God's punishment of death. (Romans 6:23)

God provided. Choose a child to read John 3:16 aloud. Say that God sent His Son, Jesus, the perfect solution to our sin problem, to rescue us from the punishment we deserve. It's something we, as sinners, could never earn on our own. Jesus alone saves us. Read and explain Ephesians 2:8-9.

Jesus gives. Share with kids that Jesus lived a perfect life, died on the cross for our sins, and rose again. Because Jesus gave up His life for us, we can be welcomed into God's family for eternity. This is the best gift ever! Read Romans 5:8; 2 Corinthians 5:21; or 1 Peter 3:18.

We respond. Tell kids that they can respond to Jesus. Read Romans 10:9-10,13. Review these aspects of our response: Believe in your heart that Jesus alone saves you through what He's already done on the cross. Repent, turning from self and sin to Jesus. Tell God and others that your faith is in Jesus.

Offer to talk with any child who is interested in responding to Jesus.

God's Plan Is Jesus

Small Group LEADER

Session Title: Jesus Was Baptized
Bible Passage: Matthew 3:13-17; Mark 1:1-11; Luke 3:21-22;
John 1:19-34
Big Picture Question: What does Jesus' baptism remind us of? Jesus'
baptism reminds us of His death and resurrection.
Key Passage: John 1:14
Unit Christ Connection: Old Testament prophecies looked forward to the
birth of Christ. Jesus' roles as Son of God and Messiah are established.

Key passage activity (5 minutes)

- Key Passage Poster
- ball

Guide kids to stand in a circle. Give one player a ball.
Direct him to say one or more words of the key passage,
and then he should pass the ball to someone else. The next
player with the ball should say one or more words and pass
the ball to someone else. Continue passing and reciting the
passage several times.

Say • Good job! Do you remember in the Old Testament
when God dwelled with His people in the tabernacle?
Jesus is God the Son, and He came to live directly
with His people.

Bible story review & Bible skills (10 minutes)

- Bibles, 1 per kid
- Small Group Visual
Pack

Option: Retell or
review the Bible
story using the
bolded text of the
Bible story script.

Review the timeline in the small group visual pack. Help
kids find Matthew 3:13-17 in their Bibles. Invite volunteers
to read the verses aloud. Then ask kids to find and read
aloud Mark 1:1-11; Luke 3:21-22; and John 1:19-34.

Say • The story of Jesus' baptism is mentioned in all
four Gospels. Does anyone know who wrote the
Gospels? (*Matthew, Mark, Luke, John*) The Gospels
tell us about Jesus' life, death, and resurrection.

Matthew, Mark, Luke, and John wrote from their own perspectives; that's why their stories aren't told exactly the same. Sometimes Matthew gives more details than Mark does. Sometimes John writes about an event in Jesus' life that Luke doesn't mention at all.

Form four groups. Assign each group one of the passages: Matthew 3:13-17; Mark 1:1-11; Luke 3:21-22; John 1:19-34. Explain that you will read a detail from the Bible story. If a group's passage includes that detail, the group should stand. If not, the group should remain seated.

Say • Jesus came from Galilee. (*Matthew; Mark*)

• God said, "This is My beloved Son." (*Matthew; Mark; Luke*)

• Jesus came out of the water. (*Matthew; Mark*)

• John tried to stop Jesus from being baptized. (*Matthew*)

• The Spirit came down like a dove. (*Matthew; Mark; Luke; John*)

Point out that the Gospels give us different details about Jesus' baptism.

Say • Let's review our big picture question one more time. *What does Jesus' baptism remind us of? Jesus' baptism reminds us of His death and resurrection.*

If you choose to review with boys and girls how to become a Christian, explain that kids are welcome to speak with you or another teacher if they have questions.

• **God rules.** God created and is in charge of everything. (Gen. 1:1; Rev. 4:11; Col. 1:16-17)

• **We sinned.** Since Adam and Eve, everyone has chosen to disobey God. (Rom. 3:23; 6:23)

• **God provided.** God sent His Son, Jesus, to rescue us from the punishment we deserve. (John 3:16; Eph. 2:8-9)

- **Jesus gives.** Jesus lived a perfect life, died on the cross for our sins, and rose again so we can be welcomed into God's family. (Rom. 5:8; 2 Cor. 5:21; 1 Pet. 3:18)
- **We respond.** Believe that Jesus alone saves you. Repent. Tell God that your faith is in Jesus. (Rom. 10:9-10,13)

Activity choice (10 minutes)

Option 1: Twist-and-turn relay

Mark two tape lines on the floor about 15 feet apart. Halfway between the lines, mark a parallel turn-around line. Instruct half of the kids to stand single file behind one outside line and the other half to stand single file behind the other. Invite kids to play a twist-and-turn relay.

- masking tape or painter's tape

Explain the rules of the relay: The first player will walk quickly across the room. When she reaches the center line, she should turn around and walk backward the rest of the way. When she reaches the next line, she will move to the back of the line, and the first player there will begin across. Kids continue crossing and turning until everyone has crossed to the opposite side.

Say • John the Baptist was baptizing people who repented of their sins. The word *repent* means to be sorry for your sin, to turn away from your sin, and to turn toward God. When John baptized people, it was a sign that they had turned from their sin and turned toward God.

- Baptism today is a little different. It is a sign that we have repented and that we trust in Jesus as Lord and Savior.

- *What does Jesus' baptism remind us of? Jesus' baptism reminds us of His death and resurrection.*

- Because Jesus died on the cross and was raised from the dead, we can repent and trust in Him and God will forgive our sins.

Option 2: A sign of something else

- large pieces of paper
- markers

Form three groups and assign each group a Bible passage.
- Group 1: Matthew 3:13-14
- Group 2: Matthew 3:15; Mark 1:9
- Group 3: Matthew 3:16-17; Mark 1:10-11; Luke 3:22

Provide markers and large pieces of paper. Instruct each group to read its passage and work together to draw a picture that represents what happened in the Bible story. When kids finish, invite them to share their signs.

Say • *What does Jesus' baptism remind us of? Jesus' baptism reminds us of His death and resurrection.*

- Jesus was baptized to show us how to obey God. Today, baptism is a sign that tells people that we trust in Jesus as Lord and Savior. We turn away from sin and begin a new life—a life lived for Jesus.

Journal and prayer (5 minutes)

- pencils
- journals
- Bibles
- Journal Page, 1 per kid (enhanced CD)
- "Jesus' Baptism Crossword" activity page, 1 per kid

Instruct each kid to write about her own baptism, a time she saw a friend baptized, or any questions she may have about baptism.

If any kids in your class have received Jesus but have not yet been baptized, be available to talk with them and their parents after class.

Say • *What does Jesus' baptism remind us of? Jesus' baptism reminds us of His death and resurrection.*

Invite kids to share prayer requests. Close the group in prayer or allow a couple volunteers to close the group in prayer. As time allows, lead kids to complete the activity page "Jesus' Baptism Crossword."

Leader BIBLE STUDY

The Devil is the agent of temptation and the father of lies. After Jesus was baptized, the Holy Spirit led Him into the wilderness. Jesus fasted for 40 days, and He was hungry. The Devil said to Him, "If You are the Son of God, tell these stones to become bread."

If You are the Son of God? The Devil knew who Jesus was. He challenged Jesus to prove it. The Devil wanted to ruin God's plan of redemption which was set in motion in Genesis 3. In the garden of Eden, Satan used a seemingly innocent question to arouse doubt in Eve: "Did God really say, 'You can't eat from any tree in the garden'?" (Gen. 3:1).

Adam and Eve ate the fruit God had forbidden them to eat, and sin entered the world. Jesus came to reverse the curse, to succeed where Adam failed. The Devil's aim was to get Jesus to sin, to disqualify Him from the role of sinless Savior.

The Devil targeted Jesus in His weakness. He tempted Jesus to turn stones into bread, to put Himself in danger, and to worship him. "Go away, Satan!" Jesus replied.

Jesus did not give in to temptation. Each time Jesus was tempted, He remembered God's Word. The Bible includes several verses about temptation. For example, God does not tempt anyone. (Jas. 1:13) We can pray to resist temptation. (Matt. 26:41) When we resist the Devil, he will flee from us. (Jas. 4:7)

The writer of Hebrews said that our high priest—Jesus—can sympathize with our weaknesses because He was tested in every way we are, yet He never sinned. Jesus' actions are an example for believers, but what happens when we do give in to temptation? Emphasize to kids that we can boldly approach God's throne to receive grace to help us through temptation, and mercy and forgiveness when we sin (See Heb. 4:14-16.) We have hope because Christ died for sinners.

Older Kids BIBLE STUDY OVERVIEW

Session Title: Jesus Was Tempted
Bible Passage: Matthew 4:1-11; Mark 1:12-13; Luke 4:1-13
Big Picture Question: How did Jesus deal with temptation? Jesus
  opposed Satan by responding with God's Word.
Key Passage: John 1:14
Unit Christ Connection: Old Testament prophecies looked forward to the
  birth of Christ. Jesus' roles as Son of God and Messiah are established.

Small Group Opening

Welcome time ....Page 198
Activity page (5 minutes)...Page 198
Session starter (10 minutes) ....Page 198

Large Group Leader

Countdown...Page 200
Introduce the session (3 minutes) ....Page 200
Timeline map (1 minute)..Page 200
Big picture question (1 minute) ....Page 201
Tell the Bible story (10 minutes) ....Page 201
The Gospel: God's Plan for Me (optional) ....Page 203
Key passage (5 minutes) ....Page 203
Discussion starter video (4 minutes)...Page 203
Sing (3 minutes)...Page 204
Prayer (2 minutes)..Page 204

Small Group Leader

Key passage activity (5 minutes) ....Page 206
Bible story review & Bible skills (10 minutes)...............................Page 206
Activity choice (10 minutes)..Page 208
Journal and prayer (5 minutes) ....Page 209

The BIBLE STORY

Jesus Was Tempted
Matthew 4:1-11; Mark 1:12-13; Luke 4:1-13

After Jesus was baptized, He was led by God's Spirit into the wilderness to be tempted by the Devil. Jesus fasted for 40 days and 40 nights. He was in the wilderness with wild animals, and He **prayed and thought about God's plan for His life. Jesus did not eat anything during those days. When those days were over, Jesus was hungry.**

Then the Devil, who tempts people to sin, **came up to Jesus.** He knew Jesus was hungry, so **he said, "If You are really God's Son, prove it. Tell these stones to become bread."**

If Jesus used His power to turn the stones into bread, He could eat them so He wouldn't be hungry anymore. **But Jesus refused. Instead of using His own power, Jesus chose to trust God to meet His needs. Jesus said, "It is written: Man must not live on bread alone but on every word that comes from the mouth of God."**

When Jesus did not give in to this temptation, **the Devil tempted Jesus again. He took Jesus** to Jerusalem, which was called the holy city. The Devil took Jesus up **to the top of the temple.** Jesus stood on the roof, and **the Devil said, "If You are really God's Son, prove it. Jump off this temple and trust God to protect You."**

Then the Devil said these words from the Bible: "It is written: God will order His angels to keep You safe, and they will protect You so that You will not even strike your foot against a stone."

The Devil had used words from Scripture, but Jesus knew the Devil's command was foolish. Jesus reminded him, "It is also written: Do not test the Lord your God."

Finally, the Devil took Jesus to a high mountain. He showed Jesus all the kingdoms of the world and how great they were. **The Devil said to Jesus, "I will give you all the riches and power of these kingdoms. They belong to me, and I can give them to anyone I want. If You want them, all You have to do is fall down and worship me."**

Jesus resisted temptation again. He **replied, "Go away, Satan! For it is written: Worship the Lord your God and serve Him only."** So Jesus wasn't going to worship anyone but God.

The Devil left Jesus, and angels came right away and began to serve Jesus. Throughout all these temptations, Jesus never sinned.

Christ Connection: Jesus was tempted, but He never sinned. Jesus is perfect and righteous. A perfect sacrifice was required to take away sin. Jesus was that perfect sacrifice. He died on the cross to free us from sin and to give us the power to say no to temptation.

Small Group OPENING

Session Title: Jesus Was Tempted
Bible Passage: Matthew 4:1-11; Mark 1:12-13; Luke 4:1-13
Big Picture Question: How did Jesus deal with temptation? Jesus opposed Satan by responding with God's Word.
Key Passage: John 1:14
Unit Christ Connection: Old Testament prophecies looked forward to the birth of Christ. Jesus' roles as Son of God and Messiah are established.

Welcome time

Greet each kid as he or she arrives. Use this time to collect the offering, fill out attendance sheets, and help new kids connect to your group. Ask kids to share how they know whether something is right or wrong. What do they do to avoid doing things they know are wrong? What do they do when they don't feel like doing the right thing?

Activity page (5 minutes)

- "Temptation Meter" activity page, 1 per kid
- pencils

Guide kids to review each situation on the "Temptation Meter" activity page and rate each based on how hard it is to do the right thing. Choose volunteers to share which situation is most tempting. Lead boys and girls to discuss how the kid in each depicted situation could say no to temptation. What would be the right thing to do?

Say • Giving in to temptation means doing the wrong thing or making a wrong choice to get something you want. We can say no to temptation.

- sticky notes
- pencils

Session starter (10 minutes)

Option 1: "I can ... " cards
Give each kid a sticky note and a pencil. Instruct kids to write on their notes something they can physically do.

Examples: *I can touch my toes*; *I can do five push-ups*; *I can hop on one foot*; and so forth. Ask them also to write their names on the sticky notes.

Collect the cards and pencils. Read the cards one at a time, allowing the class to guess who wrote the physical feat on each card. When the performer is identified, lead kids to say, "Prove it!"

Say • In today's Bible story, Satan told Jesus to prove it. He tempted Jesus by asking Him to do things that God didn't want Him to do. Do you think Jesus did what the Devil asked? We'll find out in today's Bible story.

Option 2: The right tools

- index cards
- markers
- tape

Write the following tasks and tools on separate index cards: *wash your hair, shampoo, travel around the world, airplane, slice a tomato, knife, brush your teeth, toothbrush, mow the lawn, lawn mower.*

Give each kid a card. If necessary, make more than one set or add other tool/task pairs. Instruct kids to tape their cards to their foreheads or backs.

Challenge kids to ask each other questions to find their matches. Each tool is needed to complete one task. When all the kids are paired, check their answers.

Say • Tools are very useful in completing a task we probably couldn't do by ourselves. Hammers are used to drive nails, rulers are used to take measurements, and flashlights are used to see in the dark. Can you name any other tools and their tasks?

• Today we are going to hear a Bible story about something Jesus did. To complete this task, Jesus used a powerful tool.

Transition to large group

Large Group LEADER

Session Title: Jesus Was Tempted
Bible Passage: Matthew 4:1-11; Mark 1:12-13; Luke 4:1-13
Big Picture Question: How did Jesus deal with temptation? Jesus opposed Satan by responding with God's Word.
Key Passage: John 1:14
Unit Christ Connection: Old Testament prophecies looked forward to the birth of Christ. Jesus' roles as Son of God and Messiah are established.

Countdown

• countdown video

Show the countdown video as your kids arrive, and set it to end as large group time begins.

Introduce the session (3 minutes)

• newspapers and kid-friendly magazines

[Large Group Leader enters carrying various newspapers and kid-friendly magazines.]

Leader • Hello again! I am sure glad to see you. I'm [*your name*], and I have something to show you. See these newspapers and magazines? Do you know what my favorite part of these are? The pictures! Now, why do you think newspapers and magazines have pictures?

Yes, that's right. Pictures help tell a story. Have you ever heard the saying "A picture is worth a thousand words"? You can look at a picture and see what is going on. Pictures show details that people who speak any language can understand. Let's look at some pictures to review the Bible stories we have learned so far.

Timeline map (1 minute)

• Timeline Map

Point to each picture on the timeline as you review.
Leader • Here is our timeline map. It lists the stories we've

learned in order. So far we have learned about Jesus' childhood and the beginning of His ministry on earth. First, we learned how "Jesus Was Born" in Bethlehem. Not too long after He was born, His parents took Him to the temple to be dedicated. Then, when Jesus was 12, He went to the temple to learn and to worship God. The temple was His Father's house. Last week we heard about when Jesus met up with John the Baptist, and John baptized Jesus in the Jordan River.

Today's Bible story is called "Jesus Was Tempted." Right after John baptized Jesus, Jesus went into the desert and stayed there for 40 days and 40 nights. Then the Devil tempted Jesus.

Big picture question (1 minute)

Leader • That leads me to our big picture question. Our big picture question is, *How did Jesus deal with temptation?* First, what is temptation? Does anyone have a guess? *Temptation* is something that tries to get you to make a wrong choice or to do something that is wrong. Saying no to temptation can be really hard! Let's see how Jesus resisted temptation.

Tell the Bible story (10 minutes)

- "Jesus Was Tempted" video
- Bibles, 1 per kid
- Bible Story Picture Slide or Poster
- Big Picture Question Slide or Poster

Open your Bible to Matthew 4:1-11 and tell the Bible story in your own words, or show the Bible story video "Jesus Was Tempted."

Leader • Can anyone tell me what *temptation* is? *Temptation* is something that tries to get you to make a wrong choice or to do something that is wrong. Satan tempts us to sin because he does not want us to obey God. The Devil is against everything that God desires.

How long was Jesus in the wilderness? (*40 days, 40*

nights; Matt. 4:2) Jesus fasted; He didn't eat or drink for 40 days! You can imagine how hungry and thirsty Jesus must have been.

The Devil tempted Jesus to turn rocks into bread. Did Jesus do it? No! Then the Devil told Jesus to throw Himself off the roof of the temple. The Devil wanted to test God and see if the angels would keep Jesus safe. Did Jesus jump? No! Finally, the Devil told Jesus to worship him. He promised to give Jesus land and kingdoms. Did Jesus worship the Devil? No! Jesus knew only God deserves to be worshiped. Jesus told Satan to go away, and Satan did.

Let's answer our big picture question. ***How did Jesus deal with temptation? Jesus opposed Satan by responding with God's Word.*** Say the big picture question and answer with me. ***How did Jesus deal with temptation? Jesus opposed Satan by responding with God's Word.***

During all of this, did Jesus ever sin? No. Jesus stood up to temptation, and He remembered the Bible. The Devil wanted Jesus to sin so he could ruin God's plan to save people from sin. People who sin need a perfect sacrifice. Jesus lived a perfect life and then took the punishment for sin by dying the death we deserve on the cross. When we trust in Jesus as Lord and Savior, God forgives our sin and we can be with Him forever.

Jesus is a good example of how to resist temptation, and we can look to the Bible to help us resist temptation. But sometimes we fail, and we do give in to temptation. What then? We can ask God to forgive us. Jesus obeyed God perfectly, and He is our representative. He was perfect for us. When we sin, we can ask God to forgive us. He will.

The Gospel: God's Plan for Me (optional)

Using Scripture and the guide provided, explain to boys and girls how to become a Christian. Tell kids how they can respond, and provide counselors to speak with each kid individually. Guide counselors to use open-ended questions to allow kids to determine the direction of the conversation.

Encourage boys and girls to ask their parents, small group leaders, or other adults any questions they may have about becoming a Christian.

Key passage (5 minutes)

- Key Passage Slide or Poster
- "Grace and Truth" song

Leader • Let's say our key passage together. Have you memorized it yet?

Lead kids in saying the key passage aloud. Challenge them to recite it from memory. Point out that John said the people saw Jesus' glory. Glory belongs to God.

Leader • Why would Jesus have glory like God? Yes, Jesus is God the Son. He came from the Father to earth to save people from sin.

Lead kids in singing "Grace and Truth."

Discussion starter video (4 minutes)

- "Unit 24 Session 5" discussion starter video

Leader • *How did Jesus deal with temptation? Jesus opposed Satan by responding with God's Word.* In our own lives, we face temptation often. Check out this video. Show the "Unit 24 Session 5" video.

Leader • Have you ever been tempted to cheat at a game? Would it matter if no one noticed?

Lead kids to discuss if giving in to temptation is ever OK. Remind them that God hates sin, and when we love God, we should hate sin too. Also remind kids that everyone—except Jesus—sins, and Jesus died for our sins on the cross so we can be forgiven.

Sing (3 minutes)

• "In Jesus' Name" song

Leader • Before we sing our theme song, can anyone tell me why it was important that Jesus never sinned?

Select a couple of volunteers to respond.

Leader • Because Jesus never sinned, He could be the perfect sacrifice to pay for our sin. Like Jesus, we should do our best to resist temptation. When we do sin, though, we can look to Jesus for help and ask God for forgiveness. Let's sing our theme song together.

Lead boys and girls to sing "In Jesus' Name."

Prayer (2 minutes)

Leader • Wow, this is so great. We all sin, and we need a perfect sacrifice to take away sin. Jesus was tempted, but He never sinned. Jesus is perfect and righteous. Jesus was our perfect sacrifice! He died on the cross to free us from sin. That's the gospel, the good news!

Thanks for coming, everyone. It was good to see you. Will you come back next time? Before you go to your small groups, I'm going to close in prayer.

Pray: "Lord, thank You for Your Word—the Bible—so we can learn and remember Your promises. God, we want to obey You, but we confess that we often give in to the temptation to sin. Thank You for sending Jesus to obey You perfectly and to die in our place so we can be forgiven. We love You. Amen."

Dismiss to small groups

The Gospel: God's Plan for Me

Ask kids if they have ever heard the word *gospel*. Clarify that the word *gospel* means "good news." It is the message about Christ, the kingdom of God, and salvation. Use the following guide to share the gospel with kids.

God rules. Explain to kids that the Bible tells us God created everything, and He is in charge of everything. Invite a volunteer to read Genesis 1:1 from the Bible. Read Revelation 4:11 or Colossians 1:16-17 aloud and explain what these verses mean.

We sinned. Tell kids that since the time of Adam and Eve, everyone has chosen to disobey God. (Romans 3:23) The Bible calls this sin. Because God is holy, God cannot be around sin. Sin separates us from God and deserves God's punishment of death. (Romans 6:23)

God provided. Choose a child to read John 3:16 aloud. Say that God sent His Son, Jesus, the perfect solution to our sin problem, to rescue us from the punishment we deserve. It's something we, as sinners, could never earn on our own. Jesus alone saves us. Read and explain Ephesians 2:8-9.

Jesus gives. Share with kids that Jesus lived a perfect life, died on the cross for our sins, and rose again. Because Jesus gave up His life for us, we can be welcomed into God's family for eternity. This is the best gift ever! Read Romans 5:8; 2 Corinthians 5:21; or 1 Peter 3:18.

We respond. Tell kids that they can respond to Jesus. Read Romans 10:9-10,13. Review these aspects of our response: Believe in your heart that Jesus alone saves you through what He's already done on the cross. Repent, turning from self and sin to Jesus. Tell God and others that your faith is in Jesus.

Offer to talk with any child who is interested in responding to Jesus.

Small Group LEADER

Session Title: Jesus Was Tempted
Bible Passage: Matthew 4:1-11; Mark 1:12-13; Luke 4:1-13
Big Picture Question: How did Jesus deal with temptation? Jesus opposed Satan by responding with God's Word.
Key Passage: John 1:14
Unit Christ Connection: Old Testament prophecies looked forward to the birth of Christ. Jesus' roles as Son of God and Messiah are established.

Key passage activity (5 minutes)

- Key Passage Poster
- large pieces of paper
- markers or crayons

Provide large pieces of paper and markers or crayons. Guide kids to work together or in small groups to design a sequence of pictures or symbols to help them remember the key passage.

If kids need help, give them suggestions for key words: *Word*, book or letters; *flesh*, body or hands; *among*, crowd of people; *observed/seen*, eyes; *One and Only*, number *1*; *Son*, stick figure boy; *Father*, stick figure man; and so forth.

Say • Jesus came to earth to be with God's people. Jesus' life, death, and resurrection showed that He is God's Son. He tells us the truth about who God is.

Bible story review & Bible skills (10 minutes)

- Bibles, 1 per kid
- Small Group Visual Pack
- red paper
- green paper

Option: Retell or review the Bible story using the bolded text of the Bible story script.

Review the timeline in the small group visual pack. Help kids find Matthew 4:1-11 in their Bibles. Invite kids to read the verses aloud. Then lead kids to look at Luke 4:1-13 and Mark 1:12-13. Remind kids that the writers of the Gospels—Matthew, Mark, Luke, and John—sometimes told the same stories about Jesus' life. Today's Bible story is found in three of the four Gospels. The stories are not exactly the same, but they are all about the same event.

Form three groups. Assign a Bible story passage to each group: Matthew 4:1-11; Mark 1:12-13; Luke 4:1-13. Give each group a piece of red paper and a piece of green paper. Instruct each group to choose a representative.

Explain that you will read a sentence. Each group should look over its assigned passage. If the detail you give is included in a group's passage, the representative should hold up the green paper. If it is not, he should hold up the red paper. For each sentence below, allow a representative with a green paper to read the detail aloud from the Bible.

Say • The Spirit led Jesus into the wilderness. (*Matt. 4:1; Mark 1:12; Luke 4:1*)

• Jesus was in the wilderness for 40 days. (*Matt. 4:2; Mark 1:13; Luke 4:2*)

• Jesus was hungry. (*Matt. 4:2; Luke 4:2*)

• The Devil showed Jesus all the kingdoms of the world. (*Matt. 4:8; Luke 4:5*)

• Jesus said, "Do not test the Lord your God." (*Matt. 4:7; Luke 4:12*)

• Jesus said, "Go away, Satan!" (*Matt. 4:10*)

• The angels came to serve Jesus. (*Matt. 4:11; Mark 1:13*)

• *How did Jesus deal with temptation? Jesus opposed Satan by responding with God's Word.*

If you choose to review with boys and girls how to become a Christian, explain that kids are welcome to speak with you or another teacher if they have questions.

• **God rules.** God created and is in charge of everything. (Gen. 1:1; Rev. 4:11; Col. 1:16-17)

• **We sinned.** Since Adam and Eve, everyone has chosen to disobey God. (Rom. 3:23; 6:23)

• **God provided.** God sent His Son, Jesus, to rescue us from the punishment we deserve. (John 3:16; Eph. 2:8-9)

- **Jesus gives.** Jesus lived a perfect life, died on the cross for our sins, and rose again so we can be welcomed into God's family. (Rom. 5:8; 2 Cor. 5:21; 1 Pet. 3:18)
- **We respond.** Believe that Jesus alone saves you. Repent. Tell God that your faith is in Jesus. (Rom. 10:9-10,13)

Activity choice (10 minutes)

Option 1: It is written …

Before small group, label three baskets or buckets with separate Scripture references: *Deuteronomy 6:13*; *Deuteronomy 6:16*; *Deuteronomy 8:8*. For each verse, write phrases of the verse on several sheets of paper. Mix up the pages for each verse.

- baskets or buckets, 3
- paper
- marker

　Form three groups of kids. Give each group a set of Bible verse phrases. Kids should work together to arrange their group's verse phrases in the correct order. When they finish, instruct them to look up the references on the buckets to find which reference matches their verse. Once a group identifies its reference, players can wad up their papers and toss them into the correct bucket.

Say • *How did Jesus deal with temptation? Jesus opposed Satan by responding with God's Word.*

Review each of the verses from the Book of Deuteronomy. Point out that Jesus quoted these verses when He was tempted in the wilderness. Remind kids that the Bible tells us truths about God. When we know and remember God's Word, we can stand strong against temptation.

Option 2: Mercy and grace

- poster boards, 2
- markers

Make two posters. Write the words *mercy* and *grace* on separate posters. Invite kids to define the words. Explain that *mercy* means "not getting what you deserve." *Grace* means "getting what you do not deserve." Write the definitions on each poster. Give the following examples and instruct kids to move to the appropriate sign.

Say • Ryan was speeding in his car. The police officer gives him a warning instead of a ticket. (*mercy*)

• Cate spilled her drink all over you at lunch. Now she has nothing to drink. You give her your drink. (*grace*)

• Madison forgot to do her homework last night. Her teacher allows her to turn it in tomorrow. (*mercy*)

• Ethan's brother got angry and hit Ethan. Then he apologized. "I forgive you," Ethan said. (*grace*)

Explain that Jesus set a good example.

Say • We should do our best to resist temptation. But what if we fail and give in to temptation? Does God stop loving us? No! When we trust in Jesus, God shows us mercy and grace. We still face consequences for our sin. The Bible says that people who sin deserve to die, but Jesus died on the cross in our place. And God doesn't just say that we are not guilty; He treats us as if we always obeyed Him perfectly, just like Jesus did. One day we will live with Him forever.

Journal and prayer (5 minutes)

- pencils
- journals
- Bibles
- Journal Page, 1 per kid (enhanced CD)
- "All Tangled Up" activity page, 1 per kid

Lead each kid to write or draw about a time she gave in to temptation. How did it make her feel? What were the consequences?

Say • *How did Jesus deal with temptation? Jesus opposed Satan by responding with God's Word.*

Invite kids to share prayer requests. Close in prayer, thanking God for mercy and grace when we sin. Pray that God would help kids fight temptation. As time allows, lead kids to complete the activity page "All Tangled Up."

Leader BIBLE STUDY

In the first century, *rabbi* was a title given to a respected expert in the law of Moses. A rabbi studied the Scriptures and taught through speaking and writing. Jews wanted to honor God in how they lived, and they looked to the rabbis to instruct them in their behavior.

The word *rabbi* translates "my master." Jewish students would seek out a rabbi and ask to follow him. A rabbi would choose only a few highly promising students to be his disciples. If a student was not accepted by the rabbi, he likely returned home to learn a trade. Those chosen to be a rabbi's disciples followed him everywhere. They learned from the rabbi how to think and how to act. They trusted the rabbi, and the goal was to become just like him.

When Jesus chose His disciples, His strategy was unusual. Rather than waiting for students to come to Him, Jesus sought out His disciples among the people who followed Him. He found them working—fishing and repairing nets. Some of Jesus' disciples were introduced to Him by their friends. He approached these ordinary men and said, "Follow Me." Their response? "Immediately they left ... and followed Him" (Matt. 4:20,22).

The Twelve—Peter; James, son of Zebedee; John; Andrew; Philip; Bartholomew; Matthew; Thomas; James, son of Alphaeus; Thaddaeus; Simon; and Judas—spent time with Jesus during His ministry. Jesus taught them how to think and live in light of God's coming kingdom. He commissioned them to teach others about Him. The good news about Jesus is too great to not share with the entire world.

The call to follow Jesus is not an easy one. Jesus said, "If anyone wants to come with Me, he must deny himself, take up his cross, and follow Me" (Matt. 16:24). Jesus calls us to do the same—to surrender our lives for His purposes and perhaps even to die. "For whoever wants to save his life will lose it, but whoever loses his life because of Me will find it" (Matt. 16:25).

Older Kids BIBLE STUDY OVERVIEW

Session Title: Jesus Called Disciples
Bible Passage: Matthew 4:18-22; 9:9-13; Mark 1:16-20; 2:13-14; 3:13-19; Luke 5:27-32; 6:12-16
Big Picture Question: What does it mean to follow Jesus? Following Jesus means trusting Him, obeying Him, and telling others about Him.
Key Passage: John 1:14
Unit Christ Connection: Old Testament prophecies looked forward to the birth of Christ. Jesus' roles as Son of God and Messiah are established.

Small Group Opening

Welcome time ....Page 214
Activity page (5 minutes)...Page 214
Session starter (10 minutes) ....Page 214

Large Group Leader

Countdown ....Page 216
Introduce the session (3 minutes) ....Page 216
Timeline map (1 minute)..Page 216
Big picture question (1 minute) ....Page 217
Tell the Bible story (10 minutes) ....Page 217
The Gospel: God's Plan for Me (optional) ....Page 218
Key passage (5 minutes) ....Page 219
Discussion starter video (4 minutes)...............................Page 219
Sing (3 minutes)..Page 219
Prayer (2 minutes)...Page 220

Small Group Leader

Key passage activity (5 minutes) ....Page 222
Bible story review & Bible skills (10 minutes)...................Page 222
Activity choice (10 minutes)..Page 224
Journal and prayer (5 minutes) ....Page 225

The BIBLE STORY

Jesus Called Disciples

Matthew 4:18-22; 9:9-13; Mark 1:16-20; 2:13-14; 3:13-19;
Luke 5:27-32; 6:12-16

Jesus' ministry had begun. **Jesus traveled around, preaching about God and telling people to turn away from their sins.** People were interested in what Jesus had to say. **Large crowds of people followed Jesus around and listened to Him teach.**

One day, Jesus was walking along the Sea of Galilee. He saw two brothers: Simon—who was called **Peter—and Andrew. Peter and Andrew were fishermen**, and they were casting their nets into the sea.

Jesus called out to them. "Follow Me," He said, "and I will teach you to fish for people!" **Right away, Peter and Andrew dropped their nets and followed Jesus.**

Jesus kept walking, and He **saw two more brothers. Their names were James and John.** They were in a boat fixing nets with their father, Zebedee. **Jesus called out to them, and right away they got up**, left their father and the boat, **and followed Jesus.**

Jesus went on, and He saw a man named Matthew (who was also called Levi). Matthew was sitting at the tax office. **Jesus called out to him, "Follow Me!" So Matthew got up, left everything behind, and followed Jesus.**

Matthew hosted a big feast for Jesus at his house. A large crowd of tax collectors and sinners came to eat with Jesus and His disciples. The Pharisees saw this, and they didn't think Jesus should be friends with people who did wrong things. They **complained to the disciples and said, "Why does your Teacher eat and drink with tax collectors and sinners?"**

Jesus heard the Pharisees talking, and He said to them, "People who are healthy don't need a doctor, but people who are sick do. Go and learn what this means: I want mercy, not sacrifice. **I did not come to invite good people; I came to invite sinners to turn back to God."**

Some time later, Jesus went up to the mountain to pray. He stayed on the mountain all night and prayed to God. **In the morning, Jesus called**

for His disciples. **He chose 12 of them to be His apostles.** Jesus' apostles would work closely with Jesus.

These are the men Jesus chose: Simon (who was called **Peter**), Simon's brother **Andrew, James and John** (who were called the "Sons of Thunder"), **Philip and Bartholomew, Matthew and Thomas, James the son of Alphaeus** (al FEE uhs)**, Thaddaeus** (THAD ih uhs)**, Simon the Zealot, and Judas Iscariot** (iss KAR ih aht).

Christ Connection: Jesus taught His disciples to teach others about Him. The good news about Jesus is too great to not share with the entire world! Jesus came to save people from their sin.

Small Group OPENING

Session Title: Jesus Called Disciples
Bible Passage: Matthew 4:18-22; 9:9-13; Mark 1:16-20; 2:13-14; 3:13-19;
Luke 5:27-32; 6:12-16
Big Picture Question: What does it mean to follow Jesus? Following
Jesus means trusting Him, obeying Him, and telling others about Him.
Key Passage: John 1:14
Unit Christ Connection: Old Testament prophecies looked forward to the
birth of Christ. Jesus' roles as Son of God and Messiah are established.

Welcome time

• large piece of paper
• marker

Greet each kid as he or she arrives. Use this time to collect
the offering, fill out attendance sheets, and help new kids
connect to your group.

Invite kids to share adjectives that they believe describe a
good friend. Use a marker and large piece of paper to make
a list of their responses.

Activity page (5 minutes)

• "Fishing Net Word
Game" activity page,
1 per kid
• pencils

Instruct kids to work individually or in pairs to complete
the activity page "Fishing Net Word Game." Challenge kids
to find words in the net using letters that touch—up and
down, left and right, or diagonally. There are more than 200
possible words, such as *tend*, *open*, *rented*, and *peel*.

Say • During the time Jesus lived, some men worked as
fishermen. They took their boats into the sea and
threw their nets into the water to catch fish.

Session starter (10 minutes)

Option 1: Following instructions

Play a "Simon Says" game. Lead the group with active

instructions such as "Stand on one foot," "Raise your right hand," or "Jump three times." Preface your instructions with "Simon Says … " If you do not preface your instruction with "Simon Says … ," kids should not obey the command.

Play several rounds as time allows. Invite volunteers to take turns leading the group with active instructions.

Say • You are great at following instructions! To be a good follower, you need to be a good listener first.

• In today's Bible story, Jesus chose some men to follow Him. I wonder what type of men He chose. Do you think they were smart? Talented? Popular? Hard workers? We'll find out soon.

Option 2: Team traits

• large pieces of paper
• markers or crayons

Lead kids to work in pairs or small groups. Provide markers or crayons and a large piece of paper for each group. Instruct them to draw pictures of kids who would make good teammates for a basketball game. Kids can also write characteristics of good teammates next to their pictures. Prompt kids to consider what kinds of skills the teammate has, how tall he is, the teammate's attitude, and so forth.

Say • What makes a good teammate? Would you want to play with someone who was tall but selfish? What if a fast teammate doesn't know how to dribble? Good teammates are committed, dependable, enthusiastic, prepared, selfless, and hardworking.

• In today's Bible story, Jesus chose several men to follow Him, to be on His team. Jesus chose people to help tell others about Him. The men Jesus chose might not be the type of men you would expect for such an important mission.

Transition to large group

God's Plan Is Jesus

Large Group LEADER

Session Title: Jesus Called Disciples
Bible Passage: Matthew 4:18-22; 9:9-13; Mark 1:16-20; 2:13-14; 3:13-19;
Luke 5:27-32; 6:12-16
Big Picture Question: What does it mean to follow Jesus? Following
Jesus means trusting Him, obeying Him, and telling others about Him.
Key Passage: John 1:14
Unit Christ Connection: Old Testament prophecies looked forward to the
birth of Christ. Jesus' roles as Son of God and Messiah are established.

Countdown

• countdown video

Show the countdown video as your kids arrive, and set it to
end as large group time begins.

Introduce the session (3 minutes)

• picture frame

[Large Group Leader enters carrying a picture frame.]
Leader • Hello, hello! I'm so glad you're back. I think
I've taught you just about everything I know about
photography. I was just picking up this frame to display
my favorite photos.

Hey, now that you know so much about photography,
maybe you can practice yourselves, even when I'm not
here. You were my students, and I was the teacher, but I
think you are about ready to teach too!

Well, it's almost time for today's Bible story. It's about
Jesus and His followers—the teacher and His students.
Get ready!

Timeline map (1 minute)

• Timeline Map

As you review the previous sessions, point to each Bible
story picture on the timeline map.

Leader •Look at our timeline map. Which events from Jesus' life have we learned about so far? We started with His birth. *Why was Jesus born? Jesus was born to be God's promised Savior.* Mary and Joseph took Jesus to the temple to be dedicated. When Jesus was 12, He went back to the temple and listened to the teachers there. Jesus was an adult when He began His public ministry. John baptized Him in the Jordan River, and then the Devil tempted Him, but Jesus never sinned. Today's Bible story is "Jesus Called Disciples."

Big picture question (1 minute)

Leader •Are you ready for today's big picture question? Here it is: *What does it mean to follow Jesus?* Wow, that is a very good question. Let's listen carefully to the Bible story to find out the answer to our big picture question.

Tell the Bible story (10 minutes)

• "Jesus Called Disciples" video
• Bibles, 1 per kid
• Bible Story Picture Slide or Poster
• Big Picture Question Slide or Poster

Open your Bible to Matthew 4:18-22; 9:9-13; and Mark 3:13-19. Tell the Bible story in your own words or show the Bible story video "Jesus Called Disciples."

Leader •Jesus had begun teaching and telling people to turn away from their sin. Remember, Jesus came into the world to save sinners. He is the Savior God promised.

In those days, teachers often chose students to follow them. The students watched their teachers very carefully. They tried to be just like the teachers. Teachers didn't pick just anyone to follow them; you had to be a very hard worker, and the teacher had to think you had what it takes to be a follower.

Jesus chose His followers from a group of people no one probably ever thought was smart enough to be students. Jesus' followers were called *disciples*. Jesus

God's Plan is Jesus

chose some fishermen: Peter, Andrew, James, and John. Then He chose a tax collector named Matthew. Nobody liked tax collectors. The other men Jesus chose were Philip, Bartholomew, Thomas, James, Thaddaeus, Simon, and Judas. Yes, two of Jesus' twelve disciples were named James!

Jesus' disciples would learn from Jesus so that they could tell others the good news about why Jesus came: to save people from their sins.

That brings me to today's big picture question. *What does it mean to follow Jesus? Following Jesus means trusting Him, obeying Him, and telling others about Him.* Say the big picture question and answer with me. *What does it mean to follow Jesus? Following Jesus means trusting Him, obeying Him, and telling others about Him.*

We can follow Jesus too. We don't follow Him around and eat meals with Him like His disciples did, but when we repent and trust in Jesus, He saves us from our sin and we become His followers. We can learn about Jesus from the Bible. We can trust Him, obey Him, and tell others about Him.

The Gospel: God's Plan for Me (optional)

Using Scripture and the guide provided, explain to boys and girls how to become a Christian. Tell kids how they can respond, and provide counselors to speak with each kid individually. Guide counselors to use open-ended questions to allow kids to determine the direction of the conversation.

Encourage boys and girls to ask their parents, small group leaders, or other adults any questions they may have about becoming a Christian.

Key passage (5 minutes)

• Key Passage Slide or Poster
• "Grace and Truth" song

Leader • This is our last week for memorizing this key passage. Who can tell me what our key passage is talking about?

Choose a volunteer to explain the key passage. Another name for Jesus is *the Word*. Jesus came to earth to be with God's people. His life, death, and resurrection showed that He is God's Son. He tells us the truth about who God is.

Invite volunteers who have memorized the key passage to say it aloud. Lead the group to say the key passage together. Then sing "Grace and Truth."

Discussion starter video (4 minutes)

• "Unit 24 Session 6" discussion starter video

Leader • So according to our big picture question and answer, *What does it mean to follow Jesus? Following Jesus means trusting Him, obeying Him, and telling others about Him.* Jesus calls people to follow Him. He is a good leader. You don't want to follow just anyone. Check out this video.

Show the "Unit 24 Session 6" video.

Leader • Which candidate would you vote for? Why?

Lead kids to discuss what makes a good leader. Invite kids to share why Jesus is a leader worth following.

Sing (3 minutes)

• "In Jesus' Name" song

Leader • Stand with me as we praise Jesus for inviting us to follow Him. As we sing, think about what it means to follow Jesus. Why should we follow Him? Why is He worthy of our praise? Listen to the lyrics of the song and what they tell us about Jesus.

Ask for a couple of volunteers to lead the group in singing "In Jesus' Name."

Prayer (2 minutes)

Leader • Maybe you can share some of the photo skills you learned. More importantly, you can share with others everything you have learned about Jesus! After all, *What does it mean to follow Jesus? Following Jesus means trusting Him, obeying Him, and telling others about Him.* Jesus taught His disciples to teach others about Him. The good news about Jesus is too great to not share with the entire world! Jesus came to save people from their sin.

Close in prayer. Thank God for sending Jesus to save us from our sin. Pray that God would lead kids to repent and become followers of Jesus—trusting Him, obeying Him, and telling others about Him.

Dismiss to small groups

The Gospel: God's Plan for Me

Ask kids if they have ever heard the word *gospel*. Clarify that the word *gospel* means "good news." It is the message about Christ, the kingdom of God, and salvation. Use the following guide to share the gospel with kids.

God rules. Explain to kids that the Bible tells us God created everything, and He is in charge of everything. Invite a volunteer to read Genesis 1:1 from the Bible. Read Revelation 4:11 or Colossians 1:16-17 aloud and explain what these verses mean.

We sinned. Tell kids that since the time of Adam and Eve, everyone has chosen to disobey God. (Romans 3:23) The Bible calls this sin. Because God is holy, God cannot be around sin. Sin separates us from God and deserves God's punishment of death. (Romans 6:23)

God provided. Choose a child to read John 3:16 aloud. Say that God sent His Son, Jesus, the perfect solution to our sin problem, to rescue us from the punishment we deserve. It's something we, as sinners, could never earn on our own. Jesus alone saves us. Read and explain Ephesians 2:8-9.

Jesus gives. Share with kids that Jesus lived a perfect life, died on the cross for our sins, and rose again. Because Jesus gave up His life for us, we can be welcomed into God's family for eternity. This is the best gift ever! Read Romans 5:8; 2 Corinthians 5:21; or 1 Peter 3:18.

We respond. Tell kids that they can respond to Jesus. Read Romans 10:9-10,13. Review these aspects of our response: Believe in your heart that Jesus alone saves you through what He's already done on the cross. Repent, turning from self and sin to Jesus. Tell God and others that your faith is in Jesus.

Offer to talk with any child who is interested in responding to Jesus.

Small Group LEADER

Session Title: Jesus Called Disciples
Bible Passage: Matthew 4:18-22; 9:9-13; Mark 1:16-20; 2:13-14; 3:13-19; Luke 5:27-32; 6:12-16
Big Picture Question: What does it mean to follow Jesus? Following Jesus means trusting Him, obeying Him, and telling others about Him.
Key Passage: John 1:14
Unit Christ Connection: Old Testament prophecies looked forward to the birth of Christ. Jesus' roles as Son of God and Messiah are established.

Key passage activity (5 minutes)

- Key Passage Poster
- tape or adhesive dots
- marker
- "Grace and Truth" song

Use tape or adhesive dots to mark spots on the floor in a circle, one spot per kid. Number each spot.

Guide kids to each stand on a dot. Play the key passage song and direct kids to walk around the circle. When you stop the music, each kid must stand on a dot. Call a number at random. The kid standing on that number should say the key passage from memory. Play several rounds.

Say • Very good! I hope all of you will commit to remembering our key passage. Can anyone tell me what these verses tell us about Jesus?

• Yes, Jesus is God's Son, and He came to be with God's people. He tells us the truth about God.

Bible story review & Bible skills (10 minutes)

- Bibles, 1 per kid
- Small Group Visual Pack

Option: Retell or review the Bible story using the bolded text of the Bible story script.

Briefly review the timeline in the small group visual pack. Make a list of Jesus' disciples and display it on a focal wall. Form seven groups of kids and assign each group a Bible story passage: Matthew 4:18-22; Matthew 9:9-13; Mark 1:16-20; Mark 2:13-14; Mark 3:13-19; Luke 5:27-32; Luke 6:12-16. Lead each group to read its passage aloud.

Review the list of Jesus' disciples one at a time. Invite groups to stand if their assigned passage mentions the disciple.

Point out that some of Jesus' disciples had two names. Simon was called Peter, and Matthew was also called Levi. Two of Jesus' disciples were named James: James, son of Zebedee, and James, son of Alphaeus.

Ask the following review questions:

- What were Peter and Andrew doing when Jesus called them? (*fishing, casting their nets; Matt. 4:18*)
- What did Jesus say to the men He called? (*Follow Me; Matt. 4:18; 9:9; Mark 1:17; 2:14; Luke 5:27*)
- Who had a feast at his house for Jesus? (*Matthew or Levi, Luke 5:29*)
- Why did the Pharisees complain? (*Jesus ate with tax collectors and sinners, Luke 5:30*)
- What kind of people did Jesus say He had come to help? (*sick people, sinners; Matt. 9:12-13; Luke 5:31-32*)
- How many disciples did Jesus call to be apostles? (*twelve; Mark 3:16; Luke 6:13*)
- ***What does it mean to follow Jesus? Following Jesus means trusting Him, obeying Him, and telling others about Him.***

If you choose to review with boys and girls how to become a Christian, explain that kids are welcome to speak with you or another teacher if they have questions.

- **God rules.** God created and is in charge of everything. (Gen. 1:1; Rev. 4:11; Col. 1:16-17)
- **We sinned.** Since Adam and Eve, everyone has chosen to disobey God. (Rom. 3:23; 6:23)
- **God provided.** God sent His Son, Jesus, to rescue us from the punishment we deserve. (John 3:16; Eph. 2:8-9)

- **Jesus gives.** Jesus lived a perfect life, died on the cross for our sins, and rose again so we can be welcomed into God's family. (Rom. 5:8; 2 Cor. 5:21; 1 Pet. 3:18)
- **We respond.** Believe that Jesus alone saves you. Repent. Tell God that your faith is in Jesus. (Rom. 10:9-10,13)

Activity choice (10 minutes)

- index cards, 3
- marker

Option 1: Following Jesus scenarios

Write the words *trust*, *obey*, and *tell* on separate index cards. Form three groups. Give each group an index card. Instruct the kids in each group to work together to act out one of the ways we follow Jesus. Encourage kids to be creative in how they will present the action on their index card. Be prepared to give suggestions if needed.

Allow a few minutes for groups to practice their skits. Then invite each group to present its skit to the rest of the group. Challenge the rest of the group to identify how the skit showed following Jesus: by trusting Him, obeying Him, or telling others about Him.

Say • Those are all great examples of what it means to follow Jesus. Let's say our big picture question again. ***What does it mean to follow Jesus? Following Jesus means trusting Him, obeying Him, and telling others about Him.***

Option 2: Who's missing?

- paper plates, 12
- marker

Write the names of Jesus' twelve disciples on separate paper plates: *Peter*; *Andrew*; *James, son of Zebedee*; *John*; *Philip*; *Bartholomew*; *James, son of Alphaeus*; *Thomas*; *Matthew*; *Simon*; *Thaddaeus*; and *Judas*.

Position the plates in a three-by-four grid on the floor

and instruct kids to gather around them.

Give kids 30 seconds to study the names of Jesus' disciples. Then instruct them to face away from the plates. Turn one plate over. Invite kids to turn around and identify the missing disciple.

Play again, turning over a different plate each time. As kids learn the disciples' names, mix up the plates or turn over two plates at a time.

Say • Great job. Jesus chose twelve disciples. When He called them, Jesus said, "Follow Me." ***What does it mean to follow Jesus? Following Jesus means trusting Him, obeying Him, and telling others about Him.***

Journal and prayer (5 minutes)

- pencils
- journals
- Bibles
- Journal Page, 1 per kid (enhanced CD)
- "Timeline Review" activity page, 1 per kid

Distribute journals and pencils to boys and girls. Lead kids to write the big picture question and answer on their journal pages. Invite them to write or draw examples of trusting Jesus, obeying Jesus, or telling others about Him.

Provide kids with a few minutes to journal quietly. Then gather kids together to review the big picture question.

Say • ***What does it mean to follow Jesus? Following Jesus means trusting Him, obeying Him, and telling others about Him.***

Invite kids to share prayer requests. Close the group in prayer or allow a couple of volunteers to pray. Pray that God would call each child to follow Him and that kids would be open to receiving Jesus as Lord and Savior.

As time allows, lead kids to complete the activity page "Timeline Review."